Life of a Roadie

The Gypsy in Me

By radio personality

Ronnie Rush

ISBN: 978-1-935689-80-5

Certificate of Registration

This Certificate issued under the seal of the Copyright Office in accordance with title 17, *United States Code*, attests that registration has been made for the work identified below. The information on this certificate has been made a part of the Copyright Office records.

Maria A. Pallante

Register of Copyrights, United States of America

Registration Number

TXu 1-786-756

Effective date of registration:

December 2, 2011

Title: Life of a Roadie the Gypsy in me

Author: Ronnie Rush-1953

Backcover layout: Michael Atman
Interior layout: ePubConversions.com
Front cover concept design (stage) and book title: Ronnie Rush
Front cover photo-courtesy of Jim Case
Back cover photo-courtesy of Tom Romano

Published by Wise Media Group

Synopsis

In all of Rock 'n Roll, it was the least of all cool jobs, but everyone who did it, wanted no other job: Roadie.

No show ended or started without them; they were there hours before and hours after a concert. It paid minimum wage with no benefits. But if you toured with the right group, you were dead in the middle of history. Few Roadies write their history, their personal stories, their pain and joy. But in Ronnie Rush's book, we see a slice of Rock history that does not try to bridge all of rock 'n roll music; the words place a small stone in the foundation of the growth of one group's life and travels.

> — **Ross du Clair, Chief Engineer, *Clear Channel Radio***
> **(Sacramento, CA)**

Ronnie's top 40 songs of all time:

(In no particular order)

"All Along the Watchtower" by Jimi Hendrix

"I'd Love to Change the World" by Ten Years After

"Free Bird" by Lynyrd Skynyrd

"Cruisin'" by Smokey Robinson

"Dancing Queen" by ABBA

"Dream Lover" by Bobby Darin

"It's All in the Game" by Tommy Edwards

"Time Won't Let Me" by The Outsiders

"I'm Your Captain" by Grand Funk Railroad

"California Dreamin'" by Mamas & the Papas

"Reminiscing" by Little River Band

"Carefree Highway" by Gordon Lightfoot

"Paint it Black" by The Rolling Stones

"Reunited" by Peaches & Herb

"Rocky Mountain High" by John Denver

"Yesterday" by The Beatles

"I Just Can't Stop Lovin' You" by Michael Jackson

"After the Lovin'" by Engelbert Humperdinck

"Black Water" by The Doobie Brothers

"I Can't Tell You Why" by The Eagles

"Abraham, Martin & John" by Dion

"Do You Really Want to Hurt Me" by Culture Club

"Sailing" by Christopher Cross

"Hundred Pounds of Clay" by Gene McDaniels

"I Go to Pieces" by Peter & Gordon

"Brandy" by Looking Glass

"Wishing on a Star" by Rose Royce

"It Don't Come Easy" by Ringo Starr

"The Lonely Bull" by Herb Alpert & the Tijuana Brass

"Take On Me" by A-HA

"I Want to Hold Your Hand" by The Beatles

"Five O'clock World" by Vogues

"Fool If You Think It's Over" by Chris Rea

"In the Year 2525" by Zager & Evans

"If You Know What I Mean (Babe)" by Neil Diamond

"For the Good Times" by Ray Price

"Evergreen" by Barbra Streisand

"Dream #9" by John Lennon

"Sunshine" by John Denver

"Flashdance...What a Feeling" by Irene Cara

Here's a bonus, one that is special to me because it reminds me of when I was young and played Kick the Can, and I would actually say, just after I hit the play button on the radio, "I'm going to take you back to when I was playing Kick the Can and this song was number one: Kyu Sakamoto's 'Sukiyaki.'"

Dedication

This book is dedicated to my brother Richard.

Author's Note

I've been to hell and back and shook hands with the devil, and I'm still walking tall without the smell of smoke upon me.

-Ronnie Rush-

This book is about my experiences in the music business, starting from when I was a roadie with all the experiences I had with the artists I worked for and continuing through my times in radio until my retirement. The title, Life of a Roadie: the Gypsy in Me, describes how it was that early on, even while growing up, I had a gypsy-like personality that gave me the capacity to travel the United States.

Life of a Roadie also tells about how I grew up and who I am, the history and personality that drove me to be able to handle the road and the success I experienced. I'll be taking the reader on a true-life journey that was mostly brought on by luck, circumstance, experience, and personal drive to succeed. There are three things I have always told people when I was approached and asked for advice while I was in the music business: Never give up, never give up, never give up!

Acknowledgments

To all of those whom I met and to those who have met me, seen and unseen, known and unknown:

This book is not just about those mentioned but also about me and how it was that I was able to push ahead through adversity and at all cost in order to focus on the future and not the past. I thank my mom for the little indicators along the way while growing up, one of which was allowing me to be an explorer. And I thank my father for making sure I got a good education.

I thank all the artists who took me under their wing while I was in my late teens and that gave me an opportunity to travel and become a roadie. I thank Hamilton, Joe Frank & Reynolds/Dennison for pulling me from the pits of the abyss of the unknown artists and making me a professional, and I thank Donny and Jerry Brown for preparing me for the Big Time!

Thanks to all the radio people that know me and knew me while I pursued my radio career. You know who you are.

To all the musicians in the world that made the music I used as a personal drug to get me over the rough times in life.

To Connie, the mother of my brother's children, for always, no matter what, welcoming me into your home.

To Sister Mary Brigitte Anne and all the nuns and lay teachers at Our Lady of Lourdes.

To Father Gorman and Father Collins at Our Lady of Lourdes Church.

To Mike and Cindy, for your incredible support while working the airwaves in the Central Valley, CA.

To Rush Limbaugh, for taking time out for me when I had some questions about jocking as I was just starting out in radio.

To Los Angeles' 93 KHJ's radio station's #1 jock, MG Kelly, for listening to my radio air-check at the very beginning of my radio career.

To my program directors: Sacramento's COOL 101.1fm Jon "Jonny B" Brent, San Francisco's 610 KFRC Bob Harlow, and Los Angeles' 93 KHJ's Gerry Cagle.

To Ross F. duClair, for helping me break the ice in settling in by breaking through Cow Town's cliquish force field by giving me a job in December 1984.

To Fran La Blanc, for saying, "Ronnie, your voice," while holding your hand over your heart.

To Mike Goldman, my Jewish buddy, the true definition of a friend.

And to the editor of this book, Liana Redelfs.

TABLE OF CONTENTS

The Beginning

It's hard to believe that we all started out as helpless little babies. Rarely do we think about this unless we're seeing it happen on a television screen or walking down the hall of a hospital while visiting a sick friend and happen to pass by the maternity ward. When I look at a new baby that is just hours old, I can't help but think about the long journey of his life and the hardships he will face. I think about myself and wonder how I made it this far as an adult. Will this baby make it as far? Is this new baby going to be the president of the United States of America that saves the world? I haven't made it to president yet myself, but I have made the journey, and I'm glad to be able to share it with you. Here we go!

A Touch of Hollywood

I remember when my family lived near the San Fernando Valley (near Hollywood) when I was around 5 years old. Elvis Presley was already on the charts. My big brother Richard, who was 8 years old, had been doing auditions thanks to my father's connections in Hollywood. He did an Oreo cookie commercial and some appearances on *Sky King* and *The Jack Benny Show*. His agent once asked me to audition. I was to come from out of the hall (where I was standing) and run down and into an office to my pretend mom and say, "Mommy, Mommy, can I go to the circus, please, mommy?" Even with my brother coaxing me along, I froze up. Later on, in my teen years, I saw a video of myself and cringed; I didn't like watching myself on film.

I also have a vague memory from my childhood of our family at a party in the backyard of Donna Reed's house. Even though my parents were a working class family—Mom a manager at a plant in Glendale and Dad working on the assembly line at Lockheed Airport in Pasadena—my dad that had these Hollywood connections.

My first memory of actually meeting a celebrity comes from when I was 9 or 10 years old. There was a rumor in the neighborhood that the voice of Bullwinkle (of the TV cartoon *Rocky & Bullwinkle*, which I watched) lived right across the street from our house. So I wandered over there one day, as I did a lot of wandering in the neighborhood in those days, and I noticed the neighbor working in the garage.

I said to him, "Mister, is it true that you're the voice of Bullwinkle? Can you say something in Bullwinkle talk?"

He replied, in his Bullwinkle voice, "What is it you want me to say?"

My face filled with expression when I heard Bullwinkle actually talking to me!

I can remember, at the dinner table, my mother used to say to us kids, "Children are to be seen and not heard." But I rebelled, and when I grew up, I worked on the radio, where I was heard and not seen.

[Authors note: The Hollywood sign is more than just nine white letters spelling out a city's name. It's one of the world's most evocative symbols, a universal metaphor for ambition, success, and glamour, for the dazzling place, industry, and dream we have called H-O-L-L-Y-W-O-O-D.]

Two Quarters to Rub Together

In my early 20s, I met my Italian buddy Tommy Petrochelli, and when it came time to pay for something, all I would hear was "Ronnie, I don't have two quarters to rub together." That phrase has stuck with me throughout my life; I used it myself in the years that followed when I ended up where Tommy was, without two quarters to rub together. I've used the phrase even when I had a few bucks in my pocket just so I could remember him. Tommy was one of those few good friends one meets in a lifetime. Full-blooded Italian, a bull of a personality: You didn't mess with a guy like that. He was from New York but was giving Los Angeles a try.

I was working a day job for a moving company that moved furniture locally from house to house. I was the driver and Tommy was my helper. We had become friends, and because both of us were Italian, there was a bit of brotherhood from the get-go.

I remember that Tommy was a generous guy with his time and—if he had any—his money. I went to visit him one day, and before I left he insisted that I have dinner since he had a pot of pasta cooking on the stove. It's an unspoken Italian tradition to welcome visitors to the dinner table so that they can be fed before they go on their way. Whether the table is set or not, everyone gets invited to stay and eat.

I was later able to introduce Tommy to Danny Hamilton, the lead singer for the group Hamilton, Joe Frank & Reynolds. Some weeks after that, Tommy and I were walking down the street in Sherman Oaks when a limousine drove by, and Tommy yelled, "Danny, over here! Don't leave!" in his just kidding heavy New York accent. As people have said many times over, you can take a New Yorker out of New York (for a while, anyway), but you can't take the New York out of a New Yorker.

From hanging out with Tommy and other Italians that I would meet in my lifetime as well as those who took a liking to Italians, I learned to accept and even appreciate my own Italian heritage, which wasn't exactly common in those parts when I was growing up. It was a mixed neighborhood but I got along with everyone. I don't remember not being liked as a child compared to other nationalities; I felt neutral. I could be friends with just about anyone I wanted and it wasn't a problem with the community or public opinion.

My mother's family was from Naples and my Father's family from Sicily. Both of my parents being second-generation Italian had its advantages when it came to the spaghetti sauce recipe. It was a bonus because Dad's cooking was Sicilian and mom's cooking was from Naples, which gave the household two distinct and delicious old-world recipes that we enjoyed growing up. I learned those secret recipes and cooking from both Mom and Dad. Mom was more continental and hip than my dad, who was very old-fashioned and a typical Sicilian, very strict and set in his ways. My parents met in New York, and both were born there.

I have a pleasant memory from when I was 19 and my brother and my dad and I went to see the first *Godfather* movie (1972), which was a blockbuster in its day. We went to the walk-in movies and caught a show on the big screen. My dad and I didn't communicate like typical fathers and sons of today, but during one of the scenes where the gangsters were shooting it up, I asked my dad, "Is that really the way the Italians were in your day?"

Dad said, "Yes, son, but not so open about it."

I remember, in my late teens, when a mafia-type Italian man was visiting where I also happened to be visiting at my friend's house. As this Italian man was just about to leave, he stopped and took out a wad of money, showing me the 100s wrapped with a rubber band.

He said to me, pointing to the Benjamin Franklins, "When you have a couple of these, you're Italian!"

He peeled off and handed to me two twenty dollar bills and added, "Here, kid. Buy something for yourself" in his perfect Brooklyn accent. Things like that happen all through life, and we all simply collect our experiences, good and bad, and hope that the bad doesn't overwhelm the good and make us do something foolish.

I was born in Hackensack, New Jersey, and when I was 5 years old, our family moved to the West Coast. Mom would say it was to get away from the smog. We arrived in a town called Glendale in California, but a year later we moved to another town, Tujunga, (*pronounced* Ta-hunga) near the San Fernando valley, where most of my childhood memories would shape my life and where Bullwinkle lived just across the street from my house.

[Authors note: Singer Billy Joel, mentions Hackensack in one of his songs from 1978 called "Movin' Out (Anthony's Song)," which was a Top 20 hit.]

Kick the Can

Going back years later to the hometown where you grew up is an incredible experience. I was in my late 20s when I had this urge to go back and see where I came from and where I was presently to get a perspective. I don't know if it was my way of gauging my success, but I do remember there was a yearning to go back, as if the past was pulling on me.

When I went back to Tujunga and walked the street where my childhood home had been, the same street on which I'd spent countless hours playing Kick the Can, it was like finding a huge basket of collected things and going through them one by one. I remembered the pomegranate tree that grew right along the side of the front porch, so close you could open the front screen door, step out and make a quick left, and reach over and pick a ripe pomegranate.

About ten houses down the street, there was a grove of popular tangerine trees in a lady's front yard. Neighborhood kids would always grab a few to eat as they headed past to where the mountains began for a day hike, either all the way up to what we kids called Camel's Back or to stop midway for the pristine view of Mt. Lukens at an area known as Dead Man's Gulch. As I looked around the neighborhood, I felt such a connection of mind, body, and spirit. While taking a deep breath, I remembered the tree fort a bunch of kids built in the eucalyptus trees. Eucalyptus trees are still my favorite today.

My memories from those times before I left in my late teens come to mind automatically; I can effortlessly review those early days as if I was still right there in the center of it all, as if my mind was a time machine. I remember the house that was being built next door to us. One time, when I was about 10 or 11 years old, another curious neighborhood kid and I climbed up into the attic of the incomplete house. I fell through the insulation and was knocked out about 11 feet below after landing on my chin. From what I remember, the other kid was more freaked out than I was when I came to.

My very first girlfriend, a true California natural blond girl, lived about seven houses down, and it was on my front porch that I gave her the truest tokens of my affection: my big fuzzy dice, a keychain, and a couple other things I owned, which was all I could think of that was precious to me at the time. I was just 11 years old, going on 12, and my mom called it puppy love. I still remember hearing Sonny & Cher on the radio in the background with their #1 song across America, "I Got you Babe" (1965). I had no idea I would later meet singer and future mayor of Palm Springs, Sonny Bono, in my adult life.

I remember our next-door neighbor, Ed, who had an annoying talking parrot that would call Ed by name throughout the day. I remember playing the bongos for hours down the street at a friend's house in the same year that the instrumental tune "Wipe Out" by the Surfaris hit #2 (1963). I'll never forget the mysterious house on the corner that was covered by old, full trees and overgrown shrubs and whose tenants had the last name of Coffin. Across the street from the Coffins lived a man who was building an underground bomb shelter. A few houses closer to my crib lived the neighborhood Great Dane, a friendly and playful dog who, when he put his front paws up on my shoulders, was much taller than I. I have a ton of memories from that place and those times, such as when Mom would chase my brother Richard and me out of the kitchen with a spatula, threatening to spank us, and we hid under the bunk beds. Just before reaching the bed, my brother Richard would always push me aside to get under first and leave me to slide in second, which meant that Mom always got me when she used the top bunk bedrail to fish us out from underneath.

Mom was a strong, outgoing, and personable Italian woman, and she always worked, even from my earliest memories. She was always in a good mood while I was growing up living at home or even just visiting after I had moved out. Her laugh could be heard throughout the house when there was a crowd of friends and neighbors gathered. People don't gather the way they used to today, and I don't know why, but things are different now from the way they were when I was growing up. Maybe because not only are we older but everyone moves on in life from their old neighborhoods.

I also remember my Dad holding my first two-wheeler without the training wheels. I can still hear him running alongside me, his hand steadying the back end of the bike and then suddenly letting go, releasing me to wobble my way down the middle of the street, further instilling in me that this was *my* neighborhood. Little did I know that the street I played on would expand in my later life, stretching to every state in the lower 48 and even to the beautiful country of Canada.

It is true that there are things a son or daughter only appreciates about what their parents went through or did for the family when they are older, and parochial school is one of those things for me. The Catholic school I went to from 1st to 8th grade was Our Lady of Lourdes.

From when I was about 9 years old and in the 4th grade on, I walked the mile to and from school every day, which is probably why I maintain the habit of staying in shape even now. Some mornings, I caught a ride from someone going to my school, but every afternoon I trudged the mile up the slight slope of Apperson Street with books in tow. If it rained, there was always someone getting picked up from school so I got a ride most times.

I don't remember if I ever walked home in the rain when attending elementary parochial school, but I do have some memories of local stray dogs charging at me as I walked. It wasn't because they smelled the black and red licorice I bought at the little neighborhood store I passed each day, but there was something about me that brought them running. I probably would have been bitten at least once had I not figured out a defense strategy right away. My tactic was born out of sheer terror, which quickly told my 11-year-old brain to calculate, given the dog's distance and speed, how long I had to bend over and pretend to pick up a rock and, like pro pitcher Barry Zito of the San Francisco Giants, wind up and pitch.

My strategy worked without fail. Just as I brought the closed fist with the pretend rock forward, the dog would stop dead in its tracks, veer around, and hustle back the other way, leaving me to get back to my other strategy for getting home, time-passing, which involved counting the telephone poles ahead. Each pole I passed meant I was that much closer to getting to 10326 Pinyon Avenue, the house on the street I loved and knew like the back of my hand.

At school, the nuns always asked the students to bring in books of Blue Chip stamps. The Blue Chip stamp had real value back in those days. The nuns were eventually able to use the Blue Chip stamps we brought in to buy a brand new car, a station wagon. I remember seeing a half dozen of them riding around town in their habits as they ran their errands in their new car. When I returned to the school I had attended so many years ago, the classroom seats seemed unbelievably tiny. Like the neighborhood in which I grew up, it all seemed so small.

When I was about 8 or 9 years old, I jumped from a short hill and landed hard on a board of rusty nails with only my sandals on. I remember my mother standing right there as I cried while soaking my feet in a bucket of vinegar, waiting for our family doctor to arrive and administer a tetanus shot. Doctor Mahauld was the same lady doctor who had cared for us kids ever since I can remember and who also came to the house when I had the measles. (Yes, I lived back in the days when doctors went to homes to treat patients.)

I personally feel that Catholic school may have been a hindrance to me in achieving ultimate heights in life because there were so many limitations. There was the rosary, the Ten Commandments, and Jesus watching your every move (as the nuns would preach in class) at least compared to other religions like Judaism, which seemed to be the chosen faith for all of Hollywood. The Jews there were obviously very successful and very cliquish to boot, and they helped their own. Nevertheless, I was proud to carry my Italian name.

Disadvantages aside, when I look back, I can say that parochial school was a great foundation that helped me get through some tough times later in my life. When I heard about the scandal involving Catholic priests on the East Coast, it turned my stomach. I was an altar boy on the West Coast and don't ever recall an inkling of the things that were purported in the worldwide scandal regarding my church.

Even though, as I got older, I was always studying other cultures and religions, I always thought highly of the Catholic Church. I even considered being a priest, but I wanted to travel the country, see the sights, and meet other people and cultures. And then there was my love for women. Besides, I couldn't get the hang of Latin but for a few words. When the priest asked me, just before I was to serve in the next Mass, to recite one of the prayers in Latin, I could only ever recite the first line. So it was unlikely I would have been able to serve Mass as a priest anyway, because back then it was all done in Latin, unlike now when it's done in English.

So by fate or chance, the *Monsignor* had decided early on that going beyond altar boy was not in the cards for my religious life, yet I have always carried the Catholic spirit with me, even into adult life. It seemed to me that there was a holiness about the priests and nuns and the history of the church regarding miracles that were deemed true, such as Our Lady of Fatima, where three Portuguese children were spoken to by the Blessed Mother. One of the three children later became a nun, Sister Mary Lucia. I've read both of her books, *Fatima in Lucia's Own Words* and *Fatima in Lucia's Own Words Volume 2*, which describe her experience. Her becoming a nun made me feel even closer to the belief that there was a vision. In fact, in Portugal at Fatima, on October 13, 1917, "the miracle of the sun" occurred. It was pouring rain, and the field was soaked and muddy. People's clothes were soaked. It was cold. Then, all of a sudden, the sky opened up. The sun came out. People's clothes dried immediately. The ground dried up immediately. People could look directly into the sun. It was spinning, swirling and pulsating. It appeared to be coming towards the ground. Some were terrified at times. This started and stopped three times. It could not be denied. People who were lame were able to walk, and others regained their sight. There were not just a few people in attendance. There were at least 50,000 people in the field and another 20,000 in the surrounding town, so at least 70,000 people witnessed "the miracle of the sun" that day. Even the secular newspapers had to acknowledge the miracle.

Aside from putting us in Catholic school, my folks bought a two-bedroom house with a den and a big backyard and we had a dog we called Fuzzy, all of which, collectively is, in my opinion, a solid foundation to be brought up on. I know that many of today's kids are brought up in apartments or duplexes or even on the streets. I have observed over the years that apartment life and living in duplexes doesn't seem to engender the collaboration and closeness that traditional houses in a neighborhood bring. By far, growing up in a house brings you close to the neighborhood and to playing outdoors with others.

The entrance to the mountains was easily accessed from our street. Pinyon Ave, which led up into the mountains, was just a block down the street from our house, and I grew up hiking with our dog and the neighborhood kids. We would spend days catching butterflies, hunting for snakes, and searching for caves. I still remember to this day that on some of the longer weekend hikes I ended up having to look for a small pebble to roll around in my mouth to quench my thirst when, upon reaching for the canteen on my hiking belt, I realized I was out of water. This is probably where the traveling gypsy spirit started to evolve, preparing me for the road ahead. It is true that our parents really know us from the starting gate. I remember sitting with my mom in my early 20s after she had made some spaghetti for me. We were just chatting, and then she mentioned the word *gypsy*, referring to me.

I spent my childhood on the move, playing Hide and Seek and Pony-Colt baseball on a team called the Jets, roaming all over the neighborhood, and sometimes walking or riding my bike down to the infamous Sunland Park, which was just a mile or two away.

People within a 50 mile radius knew the name Sunland Park, and many would travel to the park for outings and barbecues. The youth center was adjacent to the Teen Canteen, and I remember the dances I went to there in junior high school. I remember my first crush at the canteen and the girl I liked, though she kept her distance. I was about 14 then. One of my friends came up to me during a song by the group performing, which was playing a song by a popular group, The Vanilla Fudge, who had the hit on the radio called "You keep Me Hanging On," which peaked at #6 in 1968.

My friend said, "Ronnie, This is your song to Laura."

Yeah, more puppy love. Please, no treats for me.

On Valentine's Day, I always had a slew of cards to give to the girls. Crushes abounded. There was one time in fourth grade when we were all lined up in the playground getting ready for the raising of the flag and the bugle call. After the flag was raised and the Pledge of Allegiance was said, it was time to file into the classroom. Just as we were starting to move forward into class, another California natural blond, Carolyn, told me she'd dreamed we got married! Yep, another Valentine's card was already in my thoughts.

My brother played guitar in a band called Spider & the Crabs that played at the Teen Canteen. Their lead singer had long, stringy blond hair. He would stand center-stage and always squirmed like Mick Jagger of the Rolling Stones.

Other times, when we weren't hiking in the mountains, we would head in the opposite direction and find an entrance that would lead to the concrete wash that ran through the city. I remember walking for miles through the Tujunga wash, making handmade torches so we could explore the circular tunnels along the sides of the wash on the way. My neighborhood friends and I would crouch and crawl into dark side holes to see how far into the tunnel we could go. Sometimes there was running water draining from them, but we still entered as long as it stayed low, keeping our feet and shoes to the sides just above the water level. Every weekend was an adventure.

Once I was sitting under a tree in Sunland Park and noticed at a distance a bunch of dudes gathered around one guy. I sat and watched as the group of guys suddenly started kicking the ass of the guy in the middle. It went on for 60 seconds, and then the timekeeper said *Stop!* and just like that the crowd of guys was helping up the guy they'd just beaten and gave him a big group hug. Years later, when Richard was about in his 20s, he told me that it was a gang initiation.

When my brother was 26 he had a Harley, a shovelhead, and he parked it in his kitchen. He was only about 150 pounds at 5 feet and 6 inches, but he was fearless. He had two daughters and a wife, Connie, also from Sunland-Tujunga. When we buried Richard, there were about twenty bikers and their old ladies who came to the funeral on their Harley Choppers to show their respects, which totally freaked out my Sicilian father.

Richard was the firstborn, so there may have been a connection between my dad and him because of that. I was closer to my mom, even in resemblance. Richard had that warrior personality that my dad just could not tame. He was not so much wild as he was in a class all by himself. He was very special, a dynamic person with a photographic memory.

Still to this day, when I'm shopping and the checkers at the check stand are busy scanning away the product, I'm reminded of when my brother and I had bunk beds and I would list off items of the store he worked at as a checker.

I would say "Lucern cottage cheese?"

Richard would say, from memory, "Dollar ninety-eight."

"A loaf of Langendorf bread?"

He would say, "White or wheat?"

When I ask a checker today, "How much is Lucern cottage cheese?" the checker has to scan the product and then say, "Three ninety-eight." I wonder what Richard would say of today's scanning bars. He had a beautiful mind. He was a handsome young man, and the ladies just loved Richard.

It seems to me that when I stayed in one place for any length of time, things seemed to stay the same and I was unaware of any change from the day-to-day routine. When I was across the country and I got the call from my stepdad that my brother had shot himself. I was 23 years old, and there were people gathered around me when the phone rang, all talking. Just before I answered it, I told them all, "Okay, everybody, hold it down. There might be a death in the family."

I still don't know why I intuitively said those very words, which were verified only moments later. I dropped the phone when my stepdad told me. I walked around for what I thought was hours, but only 10 minutes later I went back to the dangling receiver.

My stepdad was still there, asking, "Ronnie, where did you go?"

"I can't believe this is happening," I said. "I was just talking to Richard a few days ago and he said he was going to drive across the country and see me."

"Get here as soon as you can," my stepdad said.

When I hung up the phone, things were starting to move in slow motion. That's the best way I can describe those few days before I caught a flight home. While on the plane, after the seatbelt signs had lit up, I asked the stewardess if she could ask the pilot to phone ahead to Los Angeles and ask for Alan Dennison. When she came back, we were at 30,000 feet, and the seatbelt sign indicated that we could unbuckle our seatbelts.

She said, "The pilot radioed the tower in Los Angeles and gave them the phone number you gave me, but the tower said there was no answer." I found out later that Alan Dennison, current keyboardist for Hamilton, Joe Frank & Reynolds at the time, had unplugged his phone for the weekend. Back then people would take advantage of the "new" plug-in-the-wall cords, where you could just unplug and therefore not be bothered by a ringing phone.

Right then and there I realized I would have to deal with this on my own. I didn't have the time or the mindset to call anyone before I left; I was just trying to get to the airport where that plane ticket from home was waiting for me and then onto the plane. I was looking for some kind of comfort and support from Alan Dennison because his family was from three generations of funeral directors.

Alan had played the organ when he was young for those families that were grieving. It was 1977, and even though the group had broken up, I still felt a strong connection to all the members of the group because of my loyalty and all those years of service on the road touring. I was in a state of suspended animation from the phone call with my stepdad until I made it to my mom's house. I caught a cab from Los Angeles International Airport to her house, where I would see just what had been taken place those few days I had spent traveling. There were my mom, my sisters, and my stepdad, all in shock.

I remember just before the funeral, sitting in the hearse with my brother's casket with the side doors of the hearse open, resting my head on the top of the casket, not wanting to let go. At some point I lifted my head up and realized that everyone was waiting for me, which was uncomfortable for me since I didn't like being the center of attention. I was only 23 years old, but was time for me to let go and say goodbye to Richard. My big brother, who had always shown up like Superman when I was in any kind of danger, was now gone.

My head still heavy, I rested again on his casket, my thoughts going back to a time in my late teens when I was rooming with a few other guys who were a little bit older than I was in a house where everyone chipped in on the rent. This living on my own was all new to me and the people I was coming across were a colorful bunch of characters, but I remained grounded. Unbeknownst to me, one of the roommates was a heroin addict, and he told me one evening that if I went to sleep that night, I wasn't going to wake up.

Needless to say, I was freaked out. I was new at the house. I had never experienced this type of confrontation. I was young and had never seen this type of attitude except on TV. The man was a deranged, sick, psycho addict.

I said to the heroin addict, "Are you sure you want to go down this road?"

He persisted. "You're dead tonight."

So I went to the phone and called Richard. He was there in 20 minutes with six other bikers. You could hear them coming down the street. My brother kicked the door in and went right up to the 6-foot, 180-pound scumbag, grabbed him, and dragged him into the other room. I can almost still hear my brother's voice as he said, "Ronnie, go outside now!"

My mind brought me back to reality, the cemetery, and the people waiting on me.

I said, "Goodbye, my brother. I will never forget you."

Then I left the hearse, got up, and went to sit on one of the chairs near the hole they would lower him into. As the casket was brought out of the hearse and set over the grave, my father stood up and walked over to the grave. All of a sudden, my father collapsed and fell onto the casket. I immediately got up and went to him. I gently picked him up and set him in a chair close by.

As we all sat there while the priest read from the Bible, I was staring at the closed casket and my thoughts drifted again, this time to the times I'd visited Richard and his wife Connie, whose mom, by the way, lived just across the street from Verdugo Hills High (my Alma mater) school in the town of Sunland, while we were growing up in the town about a mile away in Tujunga. Connie could just walk across the street to her fist period class. My brother lived in Tujunga most of his life. I was the gypsy of the family, the traveler.

I remembered a time when my brother and I were sitting on his living room couch, Richard on one end and I close by in the middle. He was holding a 12-guage shotgun pointed toward the ceiling. The gun went off, and I was stunned! I couldn't hear anything except a ringing in my ears. Then Connie came into the living room.

"Goddammit, Richard, what the fuck is going on?"

The shot put a hole in the corner of the living room ceiling and wall, and we all went into the bedroom adjacent to the wall to see where it had blown clear through. My brother was surprised by the gun going off. Connie was pissed for sure. Thankfully he had the barrel facing up.

I thought back to the funeral home, where I had gone just a day earlier into the back room and asked the funeral director what had happened to my brother.

The funeral director looked right at me, square in the eye, and said, "Ronnie, your brother had enough angel dust in his system to kill an elephant."

I didn't realize the impact this drug "thing" was having on my brother. I know he partied, but not to the extent where he would not be in control.

"Why the closed casket?" I asked.

"Your brother died from a shotgun wound to the right temple."

My mind brought me back to the funeral at hand just as the priest was finishing up his sermon. Even though I was devastated from losing my only brother, I remember the bikers walking up to me one by one.

"Ronnie, we're sorry about your brother," they said. "If you ever need us, no matter where you are or how far, we'll be there."

There are no words to describe the toll my brother's death took on my mother and father. Richard was only 26 years old, my parent's firstborn, and my only brother. Like Jim Morrison, Hendrix, and Keith Moon, he was much too young to die. There would be other brother types for me in the future, but Richard and I came out of the same womb just 3 years apart.

Years later, I realized that the plane of the top-selling southern band of all time, Lynyrd Skynyrd, had crashed on October 20, 1977, a month after the death of my brother, in the swamps of Mississippi. I had met this group a few years earlier as a roadie. More on the southern rock band Lynyrd Skynyrd ahead.

Grizzly Adams' Dan Haggerty

One of the benefits of having a brother like Richard was that he knew a lot of people. Richard was special in that way; he was a natural when it came to people and everyone who met him really just genuinely liked him. I have one great memory of a time with my brother: I was just out of my teens, from what I remember, and he drove me down from Tujunga to Sunland, which was only about two miles, to the home of one of my brother's friends, Dan Haggerty, who starred in the motion picture *The Life and Times of Grizzly Adams* (1974). My brother introduced me to Dan Haggerty outside his house, in his workshop, and I remember seeing a Harley motorcycle parked just a few feet away.

My brother saw me looking at it and said, "Ronnie, Dan Haggerty built and modified this motorcycle special for the movie and loaned it out to the movie studio. A movie star by the name of Brigitte Bardot starred in it and sat on the chopper." She was a huge star then, as big as Raquel Welch. I remember thinking, *I'm touching the seat where Brigitte Bardot sat.*

Richard was a carpet layer by trade. He was so well connected and popular with his Hollywood friends that through those friends he actually installed carpet in the home of actress Barbara Eden of the TV show *I Dream of Jeannie*. Of her husband, my brother told me, "Ronnie he's the guy you watched on Saturday morning TV as Indian Chief Cochise!"

Rolling Thunder

In the weeks after my brother Richard had been laid to rest, I went to the cemetery many times to visit his grave and place a rose on his tombstone. Things were still raw for me, and all the emotions and memories that seep into the soul of a person during a tragedy were there, ripe for the picking. While driving down the winding road leaving the cemetery, I decided to stop at a juke joint and have a beer. I parked and went up the steps of the old wooden tavern and sat at the bar.

"A beer, tall bottleneck, please," I asked.

Of course, as soon as I saw a jukebox over by where the entry was, I was up off the stool in a jolt, quarters in hand. I put in enough money to hear about six songs. I was just going to sip my beer, which would make it last long enough for me to hear all the tunes.

About halfway through the songs, the bartender said, "Hey, I like your choice of music!"

I smiled back and expressed my thanks. The next moment, a loud rumbling sound came from outside. The barstool I was sitting on was vibrating, and the ground beneath my feet seemed to hum. The roar got louder, not quite drowning out the music but loud enough for me to recognize the familiar and iconic rumble of Harleys.

I asked the bartender, "Should I leave?"

He said, "Nah, you can stay. They come here once a week to meet."

No longer was the place peaceful in the solitude of just myself, the bartender, and the music, but I stayed. I didn't feel scared or threatened when the bikers came piling in endlessly either, even though there were more than 30 filling the tavern, pressed in from where the pool tables were to the bar area where they ordered their drinks. I thought about the day of the burial and how the bikers had come to console me on behalf of my brother, whom they had genuinely loved as their own brother. I wondered if any of these bikers could be some of those that said to me on that dreadful day, "We're here for you no matter where you are. No matter how far, we will be there for you." Those words have stayed with me to this very day.

The bikers respected my space. I finished my beer, and as the last song on the jukebox played, I thanked the bartender and got up to leave.

My back to him as I opened the front door, the bartender called after me, "You take care now."

As I walked to my car, I saw the reality of where I had just been when I saw all those Harley bikes parked in rows next to each other. I don't remember if I told the bartender that I had just came from the cemetery, and I don't know whether he told the Harley riders. Now, however, years later, every time I see a Harley drive by, I'm reminded of my brother Richard, who was so very special to me.

Working!

I think back now, as I write this book, that I seem to recall working most of my life. I held a job as far back as when I was 13 years old, when I cooked breakfast at the Elks Lodge. I cooked over the hot grill for sure in those days. I remember, around that same time, cooking for my family after returning home from school. My mom was such a great cook; I was lucky to have her as a mentor when it came to the basics as well as the family secret spaghetti sauce.

Well, we really had two family secret spaghetti sauces: one from my mom's side of the family and the other from my dad's side. I remember visiting my mom in my mid-20s once, and as she was cooking some Italian dish she reminisced about how I, when in my early teens, would have everything on the stove cooking when she came home and then on the table ready to eat when it was time to sit down together for the meal. My cooking must have been good because no one complained. But I will tell you that no matter how great a cook one is, food always seems to tastes better when someone else is the cook.

We were a middle-class family. Since I've worked all my life—with maybe an exception of collecting unemployment for a short time when I was in my early 20s—I feel that if you're healthy, you should work so you can eat. Staying too long on assistance isn't good because you fall to a level of complacency, and then when the unemployment money stops, you're stuck with looking for handouts. So keep on choogin', as said singer John Fogerty, lead singer of the 60s super group Creedence Clearwater Revival.

Hollywood Carwash

In my late teens, I worked at the Hollywood Carwash. (This was before the motion picture *Car Wash* was released in 1976 and before the hit song of the same name reached # 1 in 1977.) Besides the usual army recruiters who stopped by on occasion to try to sign up some of the workers—which could have been mistaken as immigration because some of the workers would disappear for a while, and then after the recruiter was gone, the workers were back on the work line and the cars would start moving along again—movie stars would occasionally drop in to get their cars washed. I remember one day I was visiting at the home of Curly, manager of the detail department of Hollywood Carwash, and in walked Bobby Day, who sang the very popular hit song "Rocking Robin," which was #2 in 1958 on Billboard's Hot 100. One of the Temptations, Richard Street, also stopped by to visit Curly one day. The carwash was in the center of Hollywood and it was a busy one at that, partially because of its location but also because we all did a great job for the customers.

I worked at the end of the line where the cars came out nice and clean, and my job was to wipe off the excess water with hand towels, a job that always got me tips. Sometimes the customers watched, and that's when I would really go at it and spend a few extra minutes making sure the car was spotless—as long as Curly, the boss, wasn't close by, as he wanted the cars wiped fast and the customer on their way out pronto. But spending a little more time on customers' cars, especially while they were watching, was a sure way to get tips, which we were allowed to keep 100%.

The general public always seemed to tip, but movie stars very rarely did. I would always give them the first-class treatment anyway because, hey, it's Hollywood! Stars like Ernest Borgnine would say hello, hand me their claim tickets, then hop in their car and drive off. It seemed like they never carried any money with them. I think even the criminals knew this, because celebrities very rarely got jumped or robbed for the money they supposedly had in bundles. I think Hollywood made a point of creating this legendary myth so that the stars would not be bothered or panhandled while out and about running their errands.

Hollywood Gas Station

Working anywhere in Hollywood is an experience: Even the stars have to go about their days, and eventually they will have to stop for gas just like the regular customers who aren't on TV or the big screen. Everybody that has a car eventually has to stop for fuel.

In 1973, I was employed by a gas station. I worked the late shift by myself back in the day when the workers at a filling station asked, "Fill 'er up?" I, as the gas station attendant, would also wash the windshield and rear window for no extra charge. This was all before pumps started reading "Full service higher dollar, Self service lower price." I was just in my teens, working at this gas station in Hollywood, when a motion picture movie star rolled in.

He said, as he was getting out of his car, "I'm tired and just got off the set. Can you fill 'er up, please?"

It was Clint Walker. Bigger than any linebacker I had ever met, he was over 6 feet tall. As I was finishing pumping the gas, I looked down and noticed that there was a huge golf ball-sized bubble on his rear, balding tire.

I said, "Mister, you have a bubble in your tire that could blow anytime."

He looked at it and agreed. "Is there any equipment I can use? I don't have a jack in my car."

I opened the whole place up for him, and he changed the tire himself and put on the spare. Then he thanked me and was gone. I thought about how I might have saved his life that night. What if he had not stopped for gas? Later, I read that back in 1971 he was involved in a freak accident at Mammoth Mountain, California, where the tip of a ski pole pierced his heart. He made an amazing recovery and was back at work filming in Spain two months later.

Smothers Brothers

The public high school I attended was famous for the comedy team the Smothers Brothers, who had gone there many years before I did. They had a TV show on CBS, and I used to watch their comedy hour while growing up as a kid, along with *Lassie* on Sunday nights and *Bonanza*, the Western. Being just 10 years old, sitting in front of the TV and watching the Beatles on the *Ed Sullivan Show* had an impact that has stayed with me. I can still hear Ed Sullivan announce on his live show, "Ladies and gentlemen, The Beatles!" In that moment, my life was totally changed.

The country was mourning the assassination of John F. Kennedy, the 35th president of the United States, and had been since late November 1963. Yet it seemed to me that as soon as Ed Sullivan introduced The Beatles on that Sunday evening, with the whole family gathered around the TV in our living room on February 9, 1964, the happiness it gave our family was enough to give the whole country a lift. From what I heard later, just about every television set was on and tuned to the popular TV program *The Ed Sullivan Show* that night. A record-setting 73 million people tuned in, making it one of the seminal moments in television history. Nearly fifty years later, people still remember exactly where they were the night The Beatles stepped onto Ed Sullivan's stage.

When the Beatles sang their first chart hit, "I Want to Hold Your Hand," which was #1 for 7 weeks in 1964, I was still only 10 years old, but I thought, *That's a Number One record!* Well, I thought my equivalent of the concept at that time and that age, but even then I knew something was happening, not only to me but to the whole country—and that was Beatlemania!

I remember the vinyl 45" records I bought every week, collecting as many songs as I could with the weekly allowance my parents gave me for the chores I did around the house and yard. The house was spic and span and the yard well groomed. It was time to spend my allowance so I could buy as much as my allowance would buy of the Beatles and other artists' music that was available in the local music store. I wore out those vinyl records and even some diamond needles on the record player from playing my favorite songs over and over. In fact, The Dave Clark 5 had a #1 hit song in 1965 called "Over and Over Again," which had nothing to do with what I or the masses were doing with the vinyl 45" records.

I think back and remember that one of the very first records I bought and listened to was The Who's "I Can See for Miles and Miles," along with another one I remember to this day playing over and over: Bob Dylan's "Like a Rollin' Stone," which topped out at #2 for two weeks on Billboard's Hot 100 in 1965. This could have been the point in time when the seed was planted and the gypsy in me started to evolve. The music was giving me a sense of freedom, and eventually I wanted to see some of the world that the music was talking about: the places, people, and the things.

One thing was for sure, the local radio stations were playing all the top 40 hits of the week over and over, 24 hours a day, 7 days a week. Radio was a way of life. Rock & roll had come onto the scene, and television and radio made it universal. Those who gravitated towards the rock & roll movement eventually could be confirmed by news reports on TV and radio.

I remember listening to the boss jocks in my early teens playing those hits on Los Angeles' 93 KHJ radio. Even when driving to the beach on the weekends, as you parked and got out of your car you could still hear the boss jocks blaring out of the radio speakers and kicking out the hits because everyone on the beach had transistor radios tuned to the big powerhouse radio station 93 KHJ. People just could not get enough of the music that was coming out of their speakers.

The 60s radio jocks became instant celebrities. Growing up, I listened to Robert W. Morgan, the Big Kahuna, and, of course, my all time favorite, the real Don Steele. This would shape the way I thought about radio later on in my life. I knew music was for me as truly as I knew I was alive. Maybe things around me were not always conducive for the happiest of times, but when I listened to the top 40 hits, I was happy, and that was real and uplifting emotion. I really never got into the drug scene like others did. For me, music was my drug, and I couldn't get enough of the Top 40 Hits.

Avenue of the Stars

I remember when I landed a job for a law firm that was located in Century City, California. Their address was on the Avenue of the Stars. Part of my job was to update the law library down the hall when the UPS or the mailman brought in the daily mail. After that, I updated all the documents for the current laws (which seemed to arrive daily) and replace them in their particular three-ring binders for the staff to back-file later, as they would need to read up on current information. Then I spent the rest of the day running for the law firm, making deposits for the stars in Hollywood whose accounts the agency processed. The weather always seemed to be just right, and walking from bank to bank with a good pair of tennis shoes was enjoyable because of the people going every which way as they walked to their destinations as well.

It was good energy to be among those folks on the street called Avenue of the Stars, looking up at all the tall buildings and then actually stepping into one of those buildings with 40 or more stories when a bank was due to make another deposit for the company. For example, one of our clients was a very famous tennis player. One day, I had to give a bank teller a deposit slip for what was a very large amount of money back in the year of 1972. It had a leaf of check paper clipped to it for $250,000. This job was a step that took me closer to the entertainment industry. I was young, in my late teens, energetic, and excited about what life lay ahead of me.

Point to Ponder

Another one of those things in life that has stayed with me for years: I was getting onto an empty elevator in Century City, and as I turned around in the elevator to face the lobby, I noticed a senior citizen approaching as the doors closed. I stuck my arm out to prevent them from shutting all the way. As the safety bar touched my arm, the doors immediately opened back up.

The lady said, "Thank you!"

"No problem," I said. "I guess I'm a little old-fashioned."

She said, "And don't you ever change!"

Rock n Roll from the ground up

An L.A. Roadie

A roadie is a member of a crew for a traveling group of musicians or other entertainers whose work usually includes setting up equipment before shows.

I read recently about the group Ten Years After that they toured without their lead singer and guitar player Alvin Lee. How is this possible? How could Journey tour without Steve Perry? Because of my outgoing personality and my ability to communicate with anyone from 8 to 80 years old, I found myself more confident and helpful to those around me when they needed help. This contributed to my getting into being a roadie. I was a hard worker and didn't focus on money too much. Wealth was not the focus, work was, and the more I worked, the more I heard, "That guy Ronnie is a hard worker." I was not in competition with anyone or anybody I worked with; I was just a hard worker. It must have been instilled in me at an early age from my parents.

I learned early on that as long as I was working a job, the money would follow. It was the love of music and the traveling that attracted me to do what I did even though it was very hard work. I just got it done!

Back when I was a teenager in Hollywood working for SIR (Studio Instrument Rentals), I got the chance to bring a Fender Rhodes to the Santa Monica Civic auditorium to set up. (A Fender Rhodes is a small portable piano that, when played, gives a sustained sound. The group Steely Dan used it a lot back then.) At the Santa Monica Civic, the opening act was Wild Turkey, which was led by the former Jethro Tull's bass player. Then the group Ten Years After came on.

Most roadies during the performance find somewhere to hang out. I was crouching stage right (from stage, facing the audience, your right is stage right) near the monitor board when the tech said to me, "Ronnie, I'll be right back."

So there I was, just a 19-year-old kid, in awe of Ten Years After, taking the stage! Alvin Lee, who is still alive while I write this, is considered by all guitar-playing musicians to be one of the greatest of all time, dead or alive. Singer and guitarist Alvin Lee started playing an intro to one of his hits, and as I was looking at him, he suddenly turned and looked right at me.

"Turn the fucking monitor up!"

It startled me for a second, but since I knew the tech had left for just a moment, I instantly decide to accommodate his request to the best of my ability. There were dozens of knobs controlling the individual on-stage monitors for the artists, but I decided to fake it. I put my hand over one of the knobs and faked turning it.

Alvin Lee nodded at me and said, "Okay!"

That was a real trip for me, to say the least. Alvin Lee and his band had, just a few years earlier, played at the Woodstock festival of 1969, and they carried that same intense energy over to the Santa Monica Civic Auditorium.

Just before the sound check, I got to meet Alvin Lee's drummer, Ric Lee, while he was adjusting his drum kit. He was very courteous and said hello.

Their bass player moved to the beat nonstop throughout the performance. What energy! There is this special time for a roadie when you get to mingle with the musicians as they feel very comfortable around you because, after all, everyone is working towards the same goal, the big show! The fans carry a frenzied energy and must be held back from the performers. Getting to be a roadie and to stand there talking to a famous musician who is about to play in front of tens of thousands of people makes you feel special because you are part of what's going on and what's getting ready to happen: SHOWTIME!

In my personal top 40 songs of all time (which I put at the beginning of the book), the Ten Years After hit "I'd Love to Change the World" (which was #40 in 1971) is right near the top. Listen carefully the next time you get a chance, and you will hear just how gifted Alvin Lee is on guitar and how talented his band is as well. I'll never understand how it is that a key player can be missing from a group and the public will continue to pay to see the act. Robert Plant, front man of the 1960's heavy metal group Led Zeppelin, for example, when Bonzo, their drummer died, ended the group's touring and went on to do solo work, unlike The Who, which continued to tour with another drummer when they lost drummer Keith Moon.

Incidentally, Ringo Starr's son Zak Starkey has been sitting in for the Who since 1994 and was also taught under Keith Moon, and you can see some of the techniques that are reflected when Zak plays the drums.

Personal Tip to Myself

I consciously made an effort early on to not go back to any job I worked once I had left, whether it was the same location or the same type of job. This kept me moving along while I was young and energetic, even if it was by working 10 different jobs in 5 or 6 years' time, which was not a popular thing to do back when I was a teenager.

But I had a sense that it was moving me forward, so I kept at it and kept working. Ruts were sometimes inescapable because money was an issue, so sometimes I got stuck keeping the money coming in even though it was not a music-related job. But knowing myself and being as driven as I was, when the opportunity came my way, the gypsy in me was ready to go back on the road. Anything in the music world was just fine for me, but a "redo" of a day job that I'd already held was to me like going backwards. As Jimi Hendrix said in concert, "Keep on pushin' straight ahead."

I realized early on in the working world that as long as you're working there are opportunities all around because you're in motion. I didn't like the idea of being unemployed and having to collect unemployment, which locks a person into a circular routine, revolving from looking for work to getting that paycheck from the unemployment office. So taking any job frees you up from the grind of having to report that you looked for work, with the reward from the paperwork trail of "looking" for a job and getting a check from the unemployment office. A person's focus after a while becomes that of complacency and lackadaisical, and before you know it you are working at not working because over time it becomes easy money.

So my personality won't allow me to get locked into a routine of getting assistance. But again, I'm only referring to when the economy is strong. When the jobs get few and far between and you need to survive and eat, then getting that unemployment check is a bit of a cushion for when you fall on hard times because of a recession. I also knew that if I were to have to go there (collecting unemployment checks), staying on too long would not look good on the resume.

You have to be creative, and when living in a big city like Los Angeles you have to accomplish something each day or else you fall behind. Keep on keeping on! Watching all the artists I've known over the years and seeing how they approached their craft by working hard, I've found that there always seems to be a payoff. If you aren't able to be that close to see an artist at his craft, you can just turn on any radio and hear the quality of work that took many hours, if not weeks or months, for that final take. It's inspiring.

Jimi Hendrix also made it in my personal Top 40 songs of all time with his hit "All Along the Watchtower," which was #20 in 1968. Back in that era, when it was really tough to get a song into the Top 40 chart, the gifted artist Jimi Hendrix could work his magic on a hit by another artist and make it another hit. It's very, very rare that an artist would attempt to touch another artist's work after it made it onto the charts, but Jimi Hendrix could take a song that was already a hit and, after he left the recording studio, shoot the song into the stratosphere!

I'm not referring to the slew of hits that were redone as elevator music or an artist redo of a hit that kept the same lyrics and musical theme. With Jimi Hendrix, the words would be the same, but Jimi would create a whole other music arrangement, and that was his genius. It was truly a loss when he left the planet on September 18, 1970, at the young age of 27 years old. Just imagine what music he would be giving us today. R.I.P., Jimi.

A Roadie for Elton John

When I was 19 years old and working for Stax Records as an executives' assistant in the beautiful area of Century City, California, I remember one particular day when an executive called me down the hall to his office and asked me if I wanted to go on the road as a roadie with Elton John. I said sure, but later that day he told me that Elton didn't want any Americans because he thought Americans were lazy.

I was a little bummed out about not going on the road, but I was more offended by the stereotype. Elton didn't want Americans on his crew because he thought we were lazy? I knew I was a hard worker, which would be proven in the years ahead when I toured the country as the sole roadie of several different groups. In his four-decade career, Elton John sold more than 250 million records, making him one of the most successful artists of all time. His 1997 single "Candle in the Wind" has sold over 33 million copies worldwide and is the bestselling single in Billboard history. I sometimes wonder, had Elton taken a chance on me, how my life would have been different. But there again fate had to step in and keep me on the trail I was currently on, which I call the poverty trail.

There just was not a whole lot of money floating around in those early days, even for some of the artists. Some of them were ripped off or were never given their royalties on time. When I finally locked into working for just one group for a length of time, a concern for the artists after they played a club gig was whether or not the owner of the club would say, "Sorry, guys, business was slow tonight. This is all I can give you."

I knew that someday I would work for musicians that had hits on the radio. It would be a matter of time because as soon as people saw me working the stage, they would say to the drummer or bass player or guitar player, "You only have one roadie? He sets up the whole band?"

The reply was always, "Yeah, he does it all, and we just stay out of Ronnie's way."

After a show I could take down an entire drum set and pack it all away in 22 minutes. I know this because the drummer for the group I was working for, unbeknownst to me, was sitting in the audience after the show once and watched me do it.

Not going with Elton's tour meant that fate had stepped in again, and I wound up working one of the biggest shows in Los Angeles that Stax records even put on called Wattstax 72 (1972). It was filmed live in concert at the Los Angeles Memorial Coliseum and later became a motion picture documentary. Yes, you can see me in the movie working as a stagehand. Also, at the very beginning, you can see me tuning a guitar as the camera rolled while the prep was being done prior to show time.

It was an all-day gig that went into the night. Stax records had all the artists on their roster perform on that special day in Los Angeles to commemorate the Watts riots from 1965. The Staple Singers, Bar-Kays, Rufus Thomas, Carla Thomas, Albert King . . . Isaac Hayes was the headliner because of the movie *Shaft* (the original) and his #1 song of the same name from the previous year, which was huge.

Late into the night, Isaac Hayes rolled up to the coliseum tunnel in a station wagon. A very light drizzle was coming down, and if I remember correctly, the station wagon was following a Rolls Royce and motorcycle escort. They pulled up to the side steps of the stage, as you can see in the documentary, and there was a pause. Then Isaac got out, and his security team eased him up the stairs and onto the stage. The theme from *Shaft* was playing as he walked to center stage, and there I was, a roadie, standing behind a guitar amp and getting a great view from the stage as a very young Reverend Jessie Jackson walked out to announce Isaac Hayes on stage.

Including myself, there were only three white people on the stage crew. It was reported that 100,000 black people came to the mega festival event. At the beginning of the festival, I watched the young Reverend Jackson announce,

"Ladies and Gentlemen, singing our black National anthem, Sister Kim Weston." I thought, *Wow, they have their own national anthem?*

That kicked off the concert event. It got pretty intense during one of the songs Rufus Thomas sang. The stage was on the 50-yard line of the Los Angeles Ram's home playing field, and during one of the big hits Rufus was singing, "Funky Chicken," people started to come out onto the field in droves. There was a chain link fence that circled the 15-foot stage, which gave room for working staff below to roam for about 25 feet before reaching the barrier. When the people started storming the field, I was crouching stage right near the drummer and thought, *Oh shit! There's going to be a friggin riot.*

The vibe was still in the air from 7 years earlier of the violence that had taken place. Even 7 years after the Watts riots had passed. The crowd making its way down gave me the impression that they were headed right for the stage, giving me and another roadie who had bleached blond hair concern for what the memory of the Watts riots that received worldwide attention that there would be another riot! I thought maybe the brothers and sisters were still pissed off, and just because I was a roadie working this show and because I was white, I might be a target of their aggressive behavior.

I decided to prepare and take cover. I asked the drummer (as he was playing "Funky Chicken") "Am I in any kind of danger? Will I make it to my 20th birthday?"

The drummer for Rufus Thomas turned to me and said, "You're cool." He then added, "They're just coming down to dance." I was relieved.

There must have been 10,000 people on the field, and a security officer in uniform immediately came out onto the stage to tell Rufus Thomas, while he was singing, to get them back into their seats. It was a very, very delicate situation for sure. Watch the documentary *Wattstax 72* to see how Rufus, before there was rap, went into a rap-type tune to tame the crowd back into their seats. On the double vinyl 33 rpm record cover, you can see me with long, black, curly hair on stage by the equipment, just behind the young Jessie Jackson and Isaac Hayes as they hold their arms and hands up high in the air.

Point to Ponder

I've wondered over the years how is it that some of the people we see as righteous tend to die horrible deaths. One example that comes to mind is the singer, songwriter and gentle-spirited human being Mr. John Denver (1943-1997), who we all know was doing a lot to bring attention to the great outdoors, not only in his documentaries but in his music as well. Another is JFK Jr. (1960-1999), who also died in a plane crash—and in the ocean to boot!

Air Guitar

There was one time when I got to sit in to play guitar for a band. I had sat in on occasion before and would jam with other bands, but that was only on the drums. I was in my late teens the very first time I was a roadie. I met this group as I was wandering around the streets, not going anywhere in particular and not knowing how life was going to unfold as I walked with no idea of what lay ahead in my life. I was like a piece of driftwood at sea, just floating along. I really had no place to live and no friends. I was just walking, wondering just what would become of my present situation. Fate's hand was on me again.

Then I heard some music in the distance, and I followed it. My feet had never stepped on these sidewalks before, but I nevertheless kept walking. Like a bright star in the night, even though it was midday, I had this sense that I was being guided to this building where the music now was more distinct. When I arrived at the front door, I listened with my ear close to the door. I could hear the group jamming to a hit song, "Yellow River," by a British trio called Christie that had been #20 on the Billboard charts a year earlier (1970).

I waited for the song to end, then knocked hard just as the last note of the guitars played. The guitar player opened the door. I went inside, and to my amazement there were these long-haired musicians that greeted me. I sat down, and they continued with their rehearsal, playing songs I heard on the radio. They took a quick break, and we all sat around and lit up a smoke and started talking. Somehow, I didn't feel alone anymore, and I thought I must have been guided right to their front door because I'd never even seen these guys before; the area I was walking in as well as my surroundings were all new to me.

Being a teenager had its advantages because I was young and open to the world and what it had to offer. I don't think today I would ever be wandering around like driftwood at sea, but today I have wisdom and experience, which holds me back from just being a wanderer. Being young has its advantages in many ways, but so does wisdom and experience.

The group was rehearsing for an upcoming 30-city tour, and they said, "Ronnie, if you're not doing anything, we'd like to hire you to roadie for us."

Of course I said yes! They just liked me right from the start. Timing also played a part because I was available to go on their tour and be their only roadie. They mainly played out-of-town gigs, so again, timing and a bit of luck were following me the day I met up with these guys. Group Therapy was the name of the four-piece band, which consisted of Glen on lead guitar, Joe on rhythm guitar, Larry on bass guitar, and Bobby on drums. They had been playing together for a while. They sounded tight and played anything that was on the radio and the usual club requests like the blues and long jams that showed off each player's talents, like Bobby doing a drum solo.

Giddy-up! Before long, we were on the road, headed to one of the gigs that would start the tour. There was a very heavy rain that day; it was very windy and the car we were riding in was an old '57 Chevy pulling a trailer with all the band equipment inside. Bobby, the 300 pound drummer, was driving since it was his car. The strong smell of carbon monoxide was coming into the back area of the car and there was no heat, which also meant that there was no defroster, so Bobby had to take an old t-shirt and wipe the inside of the windshield whenever it fogged up, which kept him busy.

Sleeping was the best means of escape for the trip. I fell asleep there in the back of the car behind the driver side, but all of a sudden, the hood of the car flipped open and totally covered the windshield! The sound of the hood hitting the frame of the windshield woke us up.

Since I could see out the side window, I knew it was dark outside and, still coming out of my sleep, my attention went to Bobby, who was frantically pounding his side of the car with his left shoulder, trying to open the door so he could see where he was on the two-lane highway. The door would not open! Pounding again and again, Bobby finally got it to pop open, and he leaned out and safely brought us, the car, and the trailer over to the side of the road. It was still raining with wind gusts, but Bobby got out and tied down the hood so we could get back on the road and make it to the gig. It was intense, but I'm sure everyone was glad that Bobby had been driving. The first few shows with the Shirelles was our way of getting acquainted, settling into the schedule, and, of course, preparing for the crowds every night, as this was an Air Force tour of the NCO clubs along the southern route of the United States.

About midway through the 30-city tour, the guitar player had to leave immediately for home two states away, so I was asked to sit in. Their firm contract showed that four musicians were to appear behind the girl group the Shirelles, with no exceptions other than death. I had set up his guitar many times before, but that night I would have to strap it on and take the place of one of the artists.

The guitarist, Glen, promised to return in a few days. Another group scheduled to be on tour, called The Drifters, would follow this same route, and we backed them as soon as the Shirelles finished up their shows with us. They'd had a huge hit years earlier called "On Broadway," which was #9 in 1963, when The Drifters had been newly formed. I was born just 10 years before "On Broadway" was a hit. Since Glen was gone, that night I strapped on his guitar.

I knew from watching the guys each night how to stand, move, and groove (that kind of thing) all the way down to moving my hand up and down the frets of the guitar. The one problem was that I didn't know how to play. The other guitarist in the band would be right next to me during the show actually playing, but only my microphone would be left on so I could walk up to it and say "Thank you, ladies and gentlemen."

With my guitar cord plugged into the amp and the amp on standby, I could strum the guitar and do all the moves without any distortion whatsoever because I could not be heard. After we did a few warm-up songs in front of the audience, it was time for the Shirelles to perform. As the ladies came out, as they had every other night, one of the Shirelles did a double-take toward the stage and looked right at me, pointed, and smiled.

I didn't realize just how famous the Shirelles were until years later when I got into radio and started playing their many hits. They had over 10 hits on the Billboard Top 40 chart. I still remember when they would do their number #1 1962 hit "Soldier Boy" during that Air Force tour. It always went over well.

About 27 years later, one of the radio jocks I worked with interviewed Doris Jackson of the Shirelles and gave me her phone number so I could call her and say hello. After the jock had done an interview with Doris, he mentioned to her that I wanted to catch up, as I had been on the Air Force tour with her some 27 years earlier.

She said, "Sure, have him call."

I called, she answered, and I told her who I was, but it was so long ago that she didn't remember me, though we did get to chat for a moment. My radio buddy Rex soon after that would call me at my home to say that Doris Jackson had passed away. Doris was the one that sang lead on "This is Dedicated to the One I Love" (#3, 1961).

Even though she didn't remember me, I remembered her. She had told me, while on that Air Force tour so many years ago, that I had "soul." There again was a moment in time that I carried with me forever. Even if the moment hadn't lasted in her memory, I'm glad I got to chat with her for those few minutes on the phone.

Anyway, back on stage on the Air Force tour, about halfway through the set, the Shirelles' guitar player turned his back to the audience to face his amp and said under his breath where only I could hear, "Ronnie, get ready to do a solo."

I was facing the audience, thinking to myself, *What is a solo?* I quickly figured it out once he started going at it. So there I was, playing air guitar to the real solo the guitar player for the Shirelles was doing. While he "slyly" had his back to the audience, I did a solo like all the famous musicians I would later see in my life, unable to believe that I was pulling it off. Unlike the time when I was a young lad and the agent was asking me to run down the hall and say "Mommy, Mommy, can I go to the circus" and froze up, this for me was more natural. I was surrounded by those who knew me and an audience enjoying the music that was coming from the stage. I don't think anyone knew except for the musicians on stage.

The song ended, and I walked up to the mic and said, "Thank you, ladies and gentleman. We're going to take a short break now."

As I hung the guitar on the guitar stand, I really felt like a guitar player. I was told many times by musicians I worked for over the years that I "was" a musician, only that I didn't play any instrument. I learned later over the years what they meant by that statement; I was a musician "like them" in every way in mind, body, and soul. It's just I didn't play an instrument. When I stepped off the stage to take that break, I walked down the hall of the venue and several people rushed up to me and said, "Wow, that was the greatest guitar solo I have ever heard!"

That was so many years ago that I don't remember too much of the conversations I had with the fans, but I do remember that my amp was not on. I must have done a great job strumming along to the music with a guitar in hand, as they say today, playing air guitar.

Voice of God?

The band Group Therapy, now backing the world famous Drifters, finally got a VW bus for touring, which replaced the old 57 Chevy in which we narrowly escaped. The VW bus also was used to pull the trailer with all the band equipment. The VW bus was brand new, straight from the dealership, with just 11 miles on the speedometer. There would be no air guitar or strapping on a real one to fill in for an artist. This was a straight-ahead, no nonsense tour. If anything was happening at the home front, it would have to wait until the tour was over.

I was to drive throughout the night after the first show. It was early morning, just before sunrise, and the roads were dry. Not everyone knows this, but if you have been on the road most of the night, it's a potentially dangerous time to be driving because the body tends to try to go to sleep—for some drivers, even while their eyes are still open.

I was driving down the road when all of a sudden, without warning, I found myself asleep behind the wheel. My eyes flew open; I woke up in a panic, not knowing how long I had been sleeping, but luckily the VW bus and the trailer were still heading in a straight line on the correct side of the four-lane highway. I looked around and counted everyone, five in all, and all were sleeping. Two were up in the front seat with me. There was a female sitting in the middle, but she was asleep also. I think she was the girlfriend of one of the players in the band. She was just on with us for a day or so until the next gig the following day. I was the only one awake.

Then I fell asleep again. This time, I heard a voice, a deep male voice like the sound of thunder, crackling my name, "*Ron!*"

Of course, that woke my ass up, but the VW bus and its trailer had already veered off the road. Their right-side tires were in the gravel of the shoulder while the rest of the left side of the VW bus and trailer remained on the highway. I immediately got control of the vehicle and got it and the trailer back onto the highway. My whole body was trembling because it could have been worse had I not heard that male voice call my name, my real name. I'd been using a nickname while on tour, and everyone had been calling me Rocky for about a year, so I hadn't heard the name Ron until the moment I was veering off the road.

Still a little freaked out about what had just happened (and all the while preparing for a tongue lashing by one of the musicians in the back, who I thought had awoken from the road noise and saw I was veering off the highway and yelled my name), I turned around while still driving to see who it was that called my name. To my surprise, no one else was awake. Everyone in the VW bus was fast asleep, even the girl.

I immediately took the next off ramp, still trembling. My right foot was shaking so badly as I applied the brake that I thought I wasn't going to be able to make the VW bus and trailer of band equipment come to a complete stop. All the muscles in my leg were tensed up. I gave it all I had to overcome the trembling and the shakiness of the foot on the brake pedal, and I was able to pull into a café parking lot and bring the VW bus to a complete stop. Whew! Jesus! I was relieved.

One of the musicians woke up and asked, "Are we stopping?"

I said, "Yeah, I'm going to get some coffee and take a break. Someone else can drive for a while."

When I got out of the car, I knew that God had called my name while I was asleep. That voice was unlike any voice I have ever heard, and the voice said the name my parents gave me, not my nickname, which is another reason why I may have been able to wake up so quickly.

I said nothing to the band about the voice that had called my name like the crackling of loud thunder. It was my own personal experience until about a year later when I met a Christian girl who told me her own story. It was so many years ago that I don't remember her name, and I don't remember anything about her other than her incredible story, which she shared with me.

We were sitting in church one evening with some other people who were gathered around and talking. The girl told me about how she and her girlfriend were riding on the river levee road one evening in her little car, driving kind of fast, when all of a sudden she heard this voice, a male voice, a deep male voice, call her name.

Can you imagine what I was thinking as she told me this?

She said she looked at her girlfriend, and at that moment she heard her name again. There was no one else in the car other than the two of them. She immediately slowed the vehicle down to a crawl, and when she on impulse turned on her high beams, there were about 12 heads of cattle on the levee road just a few feet ahead of her car. I told her my story. Had I not met this Christian girl who shared her story, which I believed, I still would have my own personal experience to reflect on, which was very real to me and did not need any explanation or verification. But having someone a year later whom I just met tell a story from a female experience of hearing a voice, a deep male voice, I went away from that experience thinking that whatever is guiding us, that guidance brought her in to cross my path to give me verification.

It's Not "What" You Know, It's "Who" You Know

Don't get me wrong, school is very important, but I realized early on in my working life that knowing people and "having connections" was vital to progress and moving forward. It seemed to me that the more people you knew, the more opportunities there were to advance from rock group to rock group. Today, they would call it networking. If you stop for a moment and look back on your life, you can probably actually see what I'm talking about. Just think of a block of time when things were good (just so you don't start trippin' on the negatives). You will see as you look back over the years that everything seemed to be connected. If you didn't know this person you wouldn't have got that job or met your spouse, etc. It's something you really don't notice as it is happening.

All that to say that it was because of the group Shoestring, with the guitarist who played with his teeth, that I was able to work with the popular band Hamilton, Joe Frank & Reynolds (H, JF&R). This would be my big break and my first roadie job working for a recording act with hits on the Billboard Hot 100 chart, my very first group that had a record label contract.

Their record label at the time was ABC Dunhill. Shoestring's members had known Joe Frank for many years, and even though Shoestring remained at club level compared to Joe Frank, they remained friends. Joe Frank called them one day to say hello and mentioned that H, JF&R needed a roadie. I was primed and ready, as I had outgrown my present position even though I had become part of the Shoestring's band and their family. They all knew this was my desire and something I had been working up to for years, so Shoestring gave Joe Frank a high recommendation of me, and not long after that we all went out to the venue where Hamilton, Joe Frank & Reynolds would be doing their next gig at Delta State College.

I think Dan Fogelberg opened the show for the headliner act, Hamilton, Joe Frank & Reynolds. Some years later, Dan Fogelberg had a song that is played along with hundreds of other Christmas songs every year called "Same Old Lang Syne" (1980). Anyway, after the show, we all went backstage and met Joe Frank and the rest of the guys in the band. I was very excited and at the same time I had a feeling that I was getting ready to be elevated to another level. It felt like going from a college football team to getting drafted to the pros.

Joe Frank, who was also Italian, said to me, "Hey, Pisano, how are you?"

Back in the old days, when Italians would greet each other, they would use that Italian expression "Pisano" as another way of saying hello. Being back stage just after a show, you could feel the energy in the air. The artists were just winding down from performing in front of thousands of screaming fans. Joe Frank was very friendly and attentive and mentioned right off to me that when their tour was over I should call him about the roadie job.

Soon after that, I was hired on as roadie for H, JF&R. Over the years, working for local groups and mingling with all the artists of the various groups playing around town gives roadies various opportunities for work. I stuck with Shoestring, and eventually their connection to other artists (in this case, the recording act Hamilton, Joe Frank & Reynolds) moved me up and into the big time. Nothing is going to come and knock on your door to get you off the couch and give you opportunities. You have to get out there into the world. Now giddy-up!

Just Back from the Road with Hamilton, Joe Frank & Reynolds with a Full Moon

My first outing with Hamilton, Joe Frank & Reynolds, their Grammy-nominated song "Don't Pull Your Love" had already been on the charts for six months in 1971, when I joined up with them. Several hits followed that landed on the top 40 charts, and we were doing a local gig in Los Angeles. They had done a performance at the Hollywood Bowl with the brother and sister act called the Carpenters, but I missed that show.

It was late when we arrived back in Hollywood, so the drummer (the tour drummer, not the studio drummer) let me crash on his couch. I was out like a light and sound asleep when, sometime after midnight, I was startled awake by a noise.

I sat up on the couch and looked directly at the open living room window, and there I saw the huge, furry, helmet-like head of a buffalo. I knew I was not dreaming as the furry head moved back and forth, the sparse light catching on the horns coming out of both sides of the head. It seemed to be trying to come in through the window, and I knew I wasn't dreaming because it kept making a rustling sound with the screen.

I got up, went down the hall, and knocked on the bedroom door where the drummer, Lonnie Castile, was sleeping and told him what was happening.

"There's someone coming through the living room window!"

The drummer said, "Oh, that's Keith Moon. Let him in and I'll be right out."

So I welcomed Keith Moon and told him that Lonnie would be out soon. I don't remember if I opened the door for him or if he was already in the living room when I came down the hall from knocking on Lonnie's door. Keith made his way over to the couch and sat while we waited, and then

Lonnie came out and the two said their hellos like it was just another day in the studio. Keith stayed about an hour, but the whole time he was visiting, he used both hands to slap time on his knees as if he was playing the drums (as drummers tend to do) while he and his friend Lonnie talked.

I was sitting on the couch as well, and I thought about a time some years back when another rock and roll group I was roadie for let me play a tune on the drums. It was during a sound check, and I happened to be sitting on the drums, doing a few riffs as I checked the tones of the drum skins and prepared for the drummer Boogie of the Shoestring to take the stool. The drummer was behind me and, unknown to me, cueing the other band members to go ahead and kick out a tune. There I was, jamming with them, but about halfway through I stopped and called it quits. Wow, rock 'n' roll is not only hard to play; it also takes a whole shitload of energy. The artists made it look so easy!

Many years later, after getting the knack for fooling around on the drums, I sat in one time at a nightclub with a local group that played Top 40 music (the hits). The bass player made the comment that I had an incredible feel and played like Beatle drummer Ringo Starr. It was a nice compliment, and had I not had all these other goals in my mind at the time, I may have mastered the art of playing. I think I thought at the time that I was too far down the road to try and take on that dedication. I liked to jam with other bands over the years, but that was the extent of it.

So this is what I was thinking about while sitting next to Keith Moon of the rock group The Who. He had just done a sold-out concert at the Fabulous Forum in Los Angeles. I also thought about one of the very first records I had bought as a teen, the vinyl 45" record called "I Can See for Miles and Miles" (#9 in 1967) and how incredible it was that the drummer for that song was sitting right next to me. Seven years later, Keith Moon passed away on September 7, 1978, one year to the day after my brother Richard.

Fate with Lynyrd Skynyrd?

Around 1974, since Hamilton, Joe Frank & Reynolds were between hits, I returned to being a roadie for the three piece group Shoestring. They had a similar set up to the lil' ole band from Texas, ZZ Top. They were not a tribute band; they played everything, blues, the top 40, and rock & roll, and when they did play a cover song of a popular band that was heard on the radio, it was just as good. They had a loyal following. Some of the loyal fans in the audience that followed them around wherever they would perform around town could be heard shouting out their favorite song names at some of the VFW shows and local dances.

I had worked for this group for a few years and was part of their family. I could set up all three artists' equipment with ease and precision, even with an audience watching. This awareness of the audience watching my every move gave me the drive to work the stage with pride. As I was the only roadie for the three-piece group and had done the same routine many times before, it became almost like a warm-up act for the group.

When the equipment truck arrived at the gig, I would get as close to the rear stage door as I could and pick up a 4 foot by 4 foot by 4 foot 150-pound Altec Lansing speaker, put it on my right shoulder, and walk right into the nightclub and set it up on the stage. I would then set the horn speaker on top of the Altec sound speaker, the same horn speaker that was borrowed by the group Jethro Tull who used them during the Atlanta Pop Festival. The Altec speaker was a bass speaker, and the horn speaker (named so because it was shaped like a horn) was for high-end sound like the treble knob in your car stereo.

Eventually I was able to tune out the audience and just go on about my business setting up for the show. My ability to catch on fast and my hard work ethic, along with the musicians showing me how, what, and where of what to do, helped me rise to the top of my game. I became comfortable with my surroundings knowing the audience was watching; some would even work their way to the stage to talk and say hello. It was always good energy coming from the fans all the time. The anticipation of the artists' arrival and the roadies working the stage always brought a vibe of excitement for what was to come.

This three-piece group I worked for, called Shoestring, had a guitar player named Jerry that played as good as Jimi Hendrix or even Stevie Ray Vaughn. Every once in a while, Jerry would drop to his knees during a solo without missing a beat and play the guitar with his teeth, doing it just like Jimi Hendrix. He didn't do it long, only for about eight bars, but his mom would find out about it and get on him about it.

She had a direct line of information because of the buzz after a show and the fact that their family owned a local restaurant. I'm sure she heard about it when the kids talked it up while they ate their burgers and milkshakes. I cooked in the restaurant's kitchen to pay for room and board and used the money I earned from being a roadie to buy clothes—back then, mostly bell bottom jeans.

A local promoter, Carl Abraham, who was preparing for an upcoming concert, was good friends with the guitarist Jerry, his brother Donny, the bass player, and Boogie, the drummer of that three-piece group. Carl had approached the group and told them that a new and upcoming Southern rock band was going to headline a show. He wanted to know if they were interested in opening the show for them. Of course, they said yes. So there we were backstage, rubbing elbows with the supporting act that would follow us just before the headliner, Lynyrd Skynyrd, took to the stage.

Looking back some 35 years later, I remember lead singer Ronnie Van Zant being barefooted and holding a bottle of Ripple wine just before he went out. These guys reminded me of some of those western movies I had seen as a kid. They were like rough riders as they all headed out to do their set. For me, it was just another gig, another day of work.

One key part of my job was to move all of my group's equipment after they played to stage right so that the next act or the headliner could just move their stuff forward, plug in, and go. I always started tearing down and boxing up the equipment I had moved out of the way earlier around the last song of the headliner, in this case Lynyrd Skynyrd's "Free Bird." As the group was performing this song (which made it into my personal top 40 songs of all time), a year before it went on the charts, I was wrapping up cords and moving the drum kit around on stage right when all of a sudden I heard the start of a triple guitar solo.

Now, remember that these are all the original musicians on stage: Leon Wilkeson, Billy Powell, Ronnie Van Zant, Gary Rossington, Bob Burns, Allen Collins, and Ed King. I stopped working instantly and went to the edge of the stage, which is about a 10 foot drop, and jumped! (The things we can do when we are in our early 20s!)

There were no seats for rock concerts back in those days, so there I was, hanging with the audience, watching in awe with everyone else as the three guitarists went at it. I had seen Edgar Winter's guitarist, Rick Derringer, and guitarist Alvin Lee of Ten Years After, but this was something I had never witnessed or even seen done before. I thought to myself that I was witnessing a part of history whose importance would only be recognized years later. As it turned out, I was right.

At the end of the show, I was offered a job to go on the road with the seven-piece band Lynyrd Skynyrd. I don't remember if it was the road manager or the band manager, but the man came up to me during the teardown.

He said, "Ronnie, I have been watching you work the stage like no other roadie. I see you setting up and tearing down the group's equipment by yourself."

I said, "Yeah, I love my job being a roadie."

"Would you like to come and work for us?"

Being asked that question by the manager of this new group called Lynyrd Skynyrd told me that I was a good roadie.

I asked, "What's the pay?"

He said, "Sixty a week and expenses paid."

Being that I had a lot going for me in my present situation with the three-piece band that I was working for at the time and being a loyal person, I turned him down. I don't remember if it was because of the money or if fate stepped in through the fact that I was already working and had no need to accept the offer. I remembered the very moment years later when I heard that their plane had crashed in the swamps of the deep South. I'm sure I would have worked my way up to assistant road manager by then. Their assistant road manager was on the plane when it went down and lost his life.

[Authors note: Continuing the tradition of not wanting to be tied down, a girl I was dating about five years after Lynyrd Skynyrd's mega hit "Free Bird" (#19 in 1975) Kay gave me a tiny, solid gold bird on a chain to wear around my neck. A few years down the road, another lady would say that the #1 hit song "He's a Rebel," by the Crystals, reminded her of me. So the gypsy in me remains!]

H, JF&R – Danny Hamilton

Danny's birthday is June 1. There are many things, too many to mention, that are fascinating to know about this group, but I'll touch on just a couple. Danny Hamilton on, lead vocals and guitar, Joe Frank Carollo on bass and vocals, and Tommy Reynolds on many instruments and vocals (and then, later, Alan Dennison on the baby grand piano, keyboard, and vocals) were the famous group Hamilton, Joe Frank & Reynolds (H, JF&R).

We had been touring the country because the #1 hit "Fallin' in Love" (1975) was getting heavy air play, and while we were on the road it was climbing the charts. The group would stop at the radio stations in the towns we were playing and do interviews and talk to a few fans that phoned in, and the jock would give some tickets way. All of this activity across the USA while performing helped the record go Gold, with over 1,000,000 sold.

On this same tour down around Oklahoma, just after the show, we all somehow wound up in a trailer that had been converted by the promoter into a dressing room for the guys. I wasn't really close to Danny at that point in the tour as Joe Frank was more of a mentor to me since I had lived with Joe Frank in west Los Angeles (about 10 blocks from the ocean) some years earlier, just after the big hit from 1971, "Don't Pull Your Love (Out)," which Joe was at one time supposed to sing lead on but that Danny ended up singing lead for and that, of course, went on to reach the Top 5 on the Billboard 100 chart.

So there we all were in the dressing room trailer, which would have been a tight fit for even three people and was downright squishy for the five of us. All the while, there was commotion going on outside because there were 100 to 150 people at the door wanting to get in to get an autograph or to touch the band's clothing, so it was a little freaky.

I ended up sitting face to face with Danny, and he said to me, "Hey, I'm Dan."

I said, "Hello, I'm Ronnie."

I heard Joe Frank calling my name just as Dan said "Ronnie, we're soul mates."

This greeting opened a dialogue between me and Danny. I was seeing Dan prior to that the way I did Elvis Presley: his voice, his mannerisms, girls screaming and crying in the front row as he sang the ballads. So now I was able to approach him, and eventually we would have conversations relating to the spiritual and philosophical things in life. I was not intimidated by Dan; it was just that his energy was that of those huge stars you see on TV or musicians equal to that of Paul McCartney of the Beatles. I was just getting to know him. Even after the years went by, he still had this light and energy.

Joe said, "Ronnie, get us out of here even if you have to cut a hole in the floor!"

I went outside, got the suburban, and backed it right up to the dressing room trailer door. They all piled in, and we drove off back to the Holiday Inn. Who would have thought that Dan, in the years ahead, would be one of my best friends? Life is what you make of it, and sometimes life makes you!

H, JF&R – Joe Frank Carollo

Joe's birthday is September 3rd. I had gotten close to Joe Frank over the years following the big hit from 1971. Joe Frank was like a brother to me even from the first moment I met him backstage when he hired me on as their roadie. The ladies loved Joe and his bass playing; they were drawn to him because of his Southern hospitality personality and his accent. Joe had a magnetism about him. He was genuine and personable.

Danny and Joe Frank were very close musically and in business matters. Joe Frank, when we were on the road, also was the road manager, and he showed me the ropes along the way. Joe always instructed that the road crew be courteous when around the public. If any of the crew got out of line while on tour, there would be a bus ticket back home for him. Joe Frank was the lead man over all, and we all followed his lead.

When Joe Frank called me in 1975 while I was living in the Midwest (because we were between hits), he played over the phone the intro to "Fallin' in Love" (written by Danny Hamilton) and asked me what I thought.

I said, "Wow! That's a number one hit!"

I only heard the intro, but that was enough for me to jump on a plane and come home. I thought, while I was on the plane looking out the window, I would be on the road with Lynyrd Skynyrd had I accepted their offer a few months earlier. Yet here I am now going back to the group I love, and they were calling me back again as their roadie! Their song "Fallin' in Love" is one of my personal Top 5 favorite intros of all time. That song would be the group's second gold record, and yes, "Fallin' in Love" (1975) went up to the top spot on Casey Kasem's American Top 40.

Another time while on tour, Joe Frank and I were walking down the sidewalk of the Holiday Inn where we all stayed. We were talking about stage setup and the night I was calling lights and had left him literally in the dark on the tune "Badman" on the *Fallin' in Love* album. As we were walking along the sidewalk of the hotel, all of a sudden a carload of girls screeched around the corner just up ahead of us, and out came a yell from the car:

"*There they are!*"

Joe Frank grabbed me by the arm, and we dashed for the closest hideout. That was my experience of how frenzied girls could be, even after a concert.

There was another time I got to witness one of the greats of all time, Chuck Berry, from backstage. Joe Frank got a call from the union saying that Chuck Berry needed a bass player. It was a last-minute thing, so only Joe and I drove over to the venue where the show was to be held. I set up the amp, and from what I remember, Chuck Berry was running late.

He finally arrived, and when he did he downed some spirits and was ready for action—and I mean *action*! Chuck Berry went out on stage like a tornado! About midway through his show, I was able to get a great view from stage left as Chuck Berry threw himself out into the audience, guitar and all, onto what is called today the mosh pit. The crowd went wild and gently moved him along over their heads until he reached the stage and finished the rest of the show. It's these kinds of events that freeze time and become memories for future review.

Another unforgettable moment was when The Miracles, Smoky Robinson's group, opened for H, JF&R. One of the members of Smokey's group went over to a juke box that was set up at stage right and put a quarter in the slot. Bam! The show began with their hit "I'm Just a Love Machine," which was #1 in 1975.

Some things we can remember in life and some things others close to us remember totally different even though they were there in that same moment in time, standing right by your side.

H, JF&R – Tommy Reynolds

I remember it just like it was yesterday: Tommy Reynolds and I were up on the slopes in Malibu, California, overlooking the Malibu beach. I don't remember if we had to carry our tools up the slope or if we just drove around until we found a place that would allow us to look out towards the ocean.

There we were, pounding away at a 55-gallon oil drum, taking turns with the big sledgehammer we used to hit it. Tommy would pound for a while, and then I would pound for a while with Tommy showing me just where the sledgehammer should connect with the steel drum. It was loud!

I was the one hammering away while Tommy took a break and drank some water when all of a sudden a sheriff car pulled up along the embankment and walked up the ridge to join us. We looked at each other, and Tommy Reynolds said to me, "Let me handle this."

The cop finally reached us at the top of the hill, and he said to both of us, "Just what the hell are you guys doing up here?"

Tommy replied, "Well, Officer, we're making a musical instrument."

The Sheriff said, resting his hands on his weapon as they all do in their listening posture, "It sounds like y'all are making a lot of noise!"

Tommy said, "Oh, no, we're really making a musical instrument."

And he meant it! The talented Tommy Reynolds was already able to play about 10 instruments on stage.

Tommy stepped up and said, "Here let me show you."

He picked up the original steel drum (the one that I would set up on stage) and as I held it, he got out his wooden sticks with rubber bands on the end and played "Hey Jude" by the Beatles, which had stayed at the top spot on Billboard's Hot 100 for nine weeks in 1968.

The cop's face was just totally amazed.

He said, "You guys have a nice day," and then he walked back down the hill to his car and drove off.

H, JF&R - Alan Dennison

Alan's birthday is December 13th.

"Never B sharp. Never B flat. Always B natural." This was said a lot by Alan Dennison, who played piano and was one of the three key members of H,JF&R. In time, his name would become part of the lineup. He was amazing to see in concert.

Alan was the cool and suave kind of guy, a true Sagittarius. He was compassionate and intense on stage when he played the Steinway baby grand piano. There were times when you got the feeling while watching him live on stage that it was a Bach or Beethoven type of performance. His mannerisms and the intensity while he played brought out a classical element.

Alan had been playing the keyboard since the age of 5. From Marion, Ohio, even early on Alan would play the organ in his hometown—that is, in his home during funerals; his family had a three-story house and his parents worked as funeral directors.

Once on tour, we somehow got booked in Alan's hometown. Every night, Joe Frank introduced all the guys in the band and told where they were from. Then Danny Hamilton, lead singer for the group, would introduce Joe Frank. After singer/songwriter Glen Campbell recorded and released his version of Danny's hit five years later, Danny would always thank Glen Campbell for recording their hit song, "Don't Pull Your Love." Danny's version of "Don't Pull Your Love" went to #4 in 1971, while Glen's version went to #27 on the pop chart in 1976. After everyone was introduced, you could hear the roar and applause from the crowd.

But the night in Alan's hometown was different. It was a much warmer reception when Joe Frank introduced Alan Dennison on keyboards from Marion, Ohio. The crowd went wild.

I was stage right and could see and hear the deafening roar of a standing ovation as they cheered on their returning hero. It was a great moment. That show was a memorable one for sure; Alan smoked the ivories that night.

He later gave us a floor-by-floor tour of the three-story house he grew up in. I don't think we went down to the basement where the embalming took place, but we did wind up on one of the levels where the caskets were. Alan, from what I remember, was fearless as he showed us around the caskets and gave us their prices like a car salesman.

Eventually, sometime after we returned from the tour, the band split up. I was devastated when the group broke up. That same year, 1976, I went to see the newly released motion picture *Rocky* starring Sylvester Stallone.

I went alone to the theater and paid the $5 to get in. If you've ever seen that movie, you'll understand why, at that screening in 1976 when I was down in the dumps, I went out to the lobby after the movie looking for the box office girl so I could give her another $5, because I was so inspired from watching that movie that I was on top of the world again. At least, I felt that way.

I read years later that Rocky—or, I should say, Sylvester Stallone—got the run around while trying to pitch his movie. They told him, "NO! Nobody is interested in the script and no one is interested in you being in the movie either."

But he persevered. Just as in the movie, Stallone went the distance. I'm sure that everyone in the country that watched the first *Rocky* felt as if they also could go the distance. Thanks, Sylvester Stallone, for making the original *Rocky* movie.

11 Avenue 27

I really miss living 100 yards from the ocean. My address was 11 Avenue 27 in Venice/Marina Del Rey. I would wake up at 2 am and walk along the sandy beach while listening to the powerful waves crashing on the shore. I hope to someday live near the ocean again.

I had a studio apartment on the ground floor and Alan lived at the top, on the third floor. Danny Hamilton occasionally stopped by to hang out, and we would spar in my apartment, as he was a third-degree black belt in karate. He moved so fast that at times you couldn't even see him move while he got three hits in. You could feel the taps of those hits, but you'd never see them coming. He always held back, though.

So many things are precious memories once time has passed and you're able to look back. We so often miss out on experiencing that appreciation while living the moment. It's a very different feeling, looking back on a moment, like hearing a favorite song that brings you instantly back to the first time you heard it.

I remember coming out of my studio apartment one day, and as I started walking up the stairs, I noticed a trail of pine needles that started at the first step. I followed each step of pine needles up the third floor, all the way to Alan's apartment. I went in, and that's when I saw the Christmas tree. Even with the high ceiling in Alan's living room, the tree was huge! That Christmas of 1975 sure was special. Alan got everyone in the group and myself a sweatshirt that read "HJF&D Team," as the line-up now was Hamilton, Joe Frank, and Dennison, which was revealed to the public when the next album came out called *Love & Conversation*. We produced a few hits off that album.

I was very young then, in my early 20s. I had to work very hard at what I did to keep up with the professionalism of things. It was hard work getting the equipment unloaded from the trucks and then getting it set up for the show, all the while, like a hawk, keeping an eye on everything down to the patch cords that ran from the amps to the guitars, which were the very last thing that were set on stage and placed on the guitar stands, plugged in and on standby, ready for the group's sound check in the late afternoon as they arrived from the hotel.

After the sound check, they ate and returned to the hotel until I called to tell them it was Showtime! All this *is* hard work day in and day out, but at the same time it was rewarding as well. People asked me, "How come you're so young and you're with H, JF&R?" As Joe Frank told me earlier, I was just as professional as the group.

Alan had replaced Tommy Reynolds, but not right away. When Tommy called and said he no longer was going to play music, I was living with Joe Frank, and I have this memory of being in the living room listening to the stereo and turning my head towards the kitchen where Joe was talking on the phone, and I saw Joe slide his back down the wall all the way down until he was sitting on the kitchen floor. The expression on Joe's face was total puzzlement.

When Joe hung up the phone, he said, "Tommy just left the group!"

Tommy moved on to do some spiritual work, which opened up a slot for a new third artist, as the group was a longtime trio. As Danny Hamilton would announce many times in concert, the only person that could ever replace Tommy Reynolds was Alan Dennison. Once Alan was part of the trio, they had their only #1 hit on Casey Kasem's America's Top 40 countdown, "Fallin' in Love," in July of 1975.

When Alan Dennison joined the group, he was that one in a million. Alan was such a class act as a man, and of course when he play the ole ivories (the 88s), the baby grand under the spotlight of the stage. His visual motions, hair flying and what was coming out of his talented fingers, gave your bone marrow the signal to give a charge through your body. Just being in the presence of such a performance was captivating, a feeling you had to try to hold as a treasured memory. He was that great; not only in person, but you can hear it in the recorded CDs.

I was captivated myself at the beginning when he joined up with Danny and Joe Frank, and I treated Alan like royalty. When Alan took out a cigarette, I was right there to light it. Joe Frank caught that habit of mine of lighting Alan's cigarette and said, "Ronnie you don't have to light our cigarettes!"

I think Alan got the message that he was welcomed by me for sure.

H,JF&R - Johnny Barado - Tour Drummer

Johnny was one of the nicest drummers I had the privilege to work for. I remember him saying frequently to me, "Ronnie, thanks for setting up my drums with such care. You are one of the top 10 roadies of America." Johnny had done a lot of touring with other artists, so I was grateful that my hard work over the years was showing.

Johnny was from one of the toughest cities in America, Detroit, but he demonstrated to those around him gentleness and respect. You could hear the excitement in his voice when he started talking about H, JF&R/D. He loved what he did for a living and he surely loved HJF&R/D. Johnny was the sideman drummer for Hamilton, Joe Frank & Reynolds/Dennison, and he was good at his craft. Johnny Barado toured with us on the road and did some memorable TV shows in Hollywood as well.

There was a serious side to Johnny when it came to show time. After I was finished with the guitar amps and keyboards, I would make my way over to the drum riser, roll the carpet out and start setting up the drums for the group's sound check. Just as they came out on stage I would be doing the final touches on the drum stands and cymbals. A quick adjustment of the drum stool that swiveled up or down and a few riffs (on the drums) then it was ready for Johnny.

I remember one time he said to me at dinner, "Ronnie, of all the roadies that have set up my drums over the years, you are the only one that has been able to set up my drums so that when I come out for a sound check I don't have to adjust anything."

I said, "Thanks, Johnny. That's a great compliment."

I knew exactly what he meant, as over the years I could set up a group's guitar and amp then head over to the drums, and even though I set up the drums many times previously the same way, the drummer would always, no matter how many years I had set them up for the drummer, sit at the drum stool and adjust the snare, cymbals, floor tom, and high hat to "fit like a glove." This is what all drummers do to settle in before a sound check, even when it was show time. So I knew what he meant.

Johnny was a considerate human being. Like many musicians I had worked for over my lifetime. So when you are out in the audience viewing how hard the roadies are working, sweating, hustling, and exuding just how much love they have for their job, it's also the love they have for the artists they are working so hard for. As much appreciation as is coming to the artists from the audience, the artists return as much of that appreciation back to us roadies.

One thing I remember about Johnny Barado from Detroit was that not only did his mannerism remind me of the great drummer Buddy Rich, but while we would be talking sometimes he would stop suddenly in his conversation and say, "Hey!" while pointing his index finger down to his tennis shoe, where his toe shoe would be tapping time.

Oh yeah, Johnny, you got the beat for sure!

The Manager - Colonel Frank Day

Years after the group broke up, I wondered many times why the groups manager didn't have the guys of H, JF&R do a Christmas song, which could have played every year at Christmas along with all the other great artists' songs for years to come. My job as roadie was to take care of the guys on the road, making sure they got from place to place. It was the manager's job to make sure the guys got their royalties, record deals, and so forth. So why didn't the manager see to it that they did a Christmas song?

To me, as young a man as I was, the group's manager carried a great deal of weight. I perceived him to be well connected in the music business. He worked out of the same plush Hollywood office as the management team of Helen Reddy, the female singer who soared up the Top 40 charts with over 14 hits, three of which made it to the #1 top spot on the Casey Kasem's American Top 40 Countdown.

There was this time when we were on tour and running a little late for a gig. It was a one-off from the usual tour; it hadn't been scheduled until we were already on the road, and we all were just about out of money. Normally, a deposit is made by the promoter months in advance, and then we collect the balance when we perform, but there was no time for prearrangement on this gig because the promoter had booked it while we were on the road. Our instructions from the group manager were to collect the whole amount, headline the show, and continue on the road after the concert to the next town. There would be no stopping at a hotel, just play and go! We were scheduled to headline the show, so the supporting act, by all accounts, would be performing as we arrived at the venue.

Joe Frank was driving the tour bus and commented, "Yeah, we're running a little late, but our record 'Fallin' in Love' just moved up the charts to number one." He added, "Ronnie, tonight you get a break because all of us will be unloading the equipment. You just make sure it is set up on stage. We'll bring you the equipment and you get it ready behind the supporting act while they're playing."

"Not a problem for me, Joe Frank," I said.

When we arrived, however, things did not go as we had planned. The supporting act had not gone up to perform.

I went to the promoter and asked, "Why isn't the supporting act on stage?"

The promoter said, "Didn't you see the marquee out front?"

The supporting act's name was printed in very large letters. Our name, "Hamilton, Joe Frank & Reynolds" was barely on there, small enough to indicate that *we* were supposed to go on first as the supporting act!

This created quite a bit of urgency because if we didn't go on we wouldn't get paid, regardless of the fact that we had the #1 record in the country.

The supporting act, when asked to go on since their stuff was already set up, plugged in, and ready to go, said there was "absolutely no fucking way we're going on first."

"We are the headliner," the road manager for the supporting act said.

So I told Joe Frank what was up, and we all unloaded the equipment and lugged it from the front entrance through the crowd and onto the stage. The piano Alan would be playing was there, but it was set up stage right, and Alan always played stage left.

The stage manager for the supporting act told us, "The piano stays right where it is."

I knew from experience that this was reasonable because once a piano is tuned, it must not be moved. But the stage manager's point about not moving it had nothing to do with my thoughts. I was fuming over the fact that I was dealing with some real assholes! They knew we were running late (in their eyes), but they would not lift a finger to help out.

H, JF&R went on and played the set, and the supposed supporting act went on after us as headliner. While they were getting started, I went into the promoter's office to get our pay, which would either be a certified check or cash. Normally, this stage of the transaction happens before the guys go on to perform, but with the confusion that ensued upon our arrival, the guys had gone on anyway.

The Amazing Rhythm Aces were performing while I was in the promoter's office asking for our payment. It's not a good situation when it's done this way. The act is usually in the dressing room waiting for word from me that they have been paid before they walk out on stage and greet the anxious crowd. If the promoter does not pay, then the group does not go on, which could cause a riot. The promoter knows this, and so it's the crowd that keeps him honest. In this fiasco, however, the guys had already played.

The promoter looked up at me from his desk and said, "I'm sorry, but you guys were late."

He had more bullshit to add, and when he was done, I said, "Are you sure you want to go down this road?"

The promoter said, "There is no money."

Right then, I picked up their office phone, and from somewhere in the Midwest, I called Colonel Frank Day, the group's manager. While the phone was ringing, I thought about how hard the group had worked over the years, even getting a Grammy nomination a few years earlier for "Don't Pull Your Love," which hit #4 on Billboard's Hot 100 chart.

Frank answered the phone from his home in Bel Air, just outside Hollywood.

Frank said, "Yes, hello."

I said, "Frank, we're in such-and-such town. Our itinerary says we were to go on as headliner, and that did not happen. We went on first, and now the promoter doesn't want to pay us."

Frank said, "Ronnie, hand the phone to John."

I passed the phone to the promoter. While they were talking on the phone, I could hear the Amazing Rhythm Aces playing out on the stage. I knew that enough time had passed that H, JF&R would have all the equipment off the stage and loaded on the bus, ready to go.

My attention went back to the promoter, whose face was looking increasingly worried as he listened to Frank. After a long few minutes, the promoter slowly hung up. He stood up from his cushy chair, and from out of his back pocket he pulled out a wad of cash and counted out the owed $5,000.00. When he finished the count, I counted it again back to him and headed out. I never asked what Frank told him on the phone. I was just glad to get the business done and go. I did notice, on my way out of the venue, that the Rhythm Aces were playing but no one had stayed for their show. The janitor was sweeping the floor.

Missing the Bus

In my younger years, I was always on the move, which was a good foundation for preparing me for the long, rugged tours that came later. When carnival acts came to town, you can see them setting up and getting things ready. The carnies always looked to me like rough riders; that's what the road did to you. It definitely took a toll on all the musicians and myself to stay out on the road. I'm not saying we looked like those carnies, but the road gave us an attitude. It's just one of those things that came with the territory.

Mick Jagger, Paul McCartney, and Billy Joel, all successful then and now, had a much easier time of traveling because they had money. For us, there was very little of it back then, which created other problems. I remember one time the tour bus we were on had stopped at a truck stop while I was asleep in the back.

The hum and the movement of the bus was a great substitute for a sleeping pill, and it could carry you off into a gentle slumber before you knew it. My body recognized the change in motion, I suppose, and I subconsciously knew the bus had stopped. I woke up, still groggy, and got off the bus to use the bathroom and get something to drink. But when I went back outside, the bus was gone!

I thought, *Shit! I have no coat, no money, and I'm in an entirely different state from the one I live in.* (I lived in Los Angeles at the time). So I thought for a minute (there were no cell phones back in those days), and then I remembered that truck drivers have CB radios and that Joe Frank was a CB nut.

We all had handles when we used the CB radio. Danny thought of his right on the spot when Joe Frank said we all should have them. Danny thought of his hit record "Fallin' in Love," and out of his mouth came the handle "Fallin' Tree." Mine was "Super Sound" because Danny had just told me a few nights earlier, when no sound guy had been available and I'd sat in, that the sound was incredible. He said, "Ronnie, people were coming up to me after the show and said that we sounded just like the album."

So I hunted down a trucker and told him what my situation was and asked if he could call on the CB radio for "Mississippi Mailman," Joe Frank's handle. I don't quite remember if I met up with the group or just rode the rest of the way home with the truck driver, as we were done with the tour and heading home anyways and the driver happened to be heading in the same direction. Some things we remember and some things we just can't, but if I were to ask one of the guys they may have some idea of what happened that night. I do remember Joe Frank saying that they had no idea I had even gotten off the bus.

Familiar

We all have experienced it sometime or another, with someone you have become friends with or a loved one that you haven't seen in awhile, where all of a sudden there is a complete stranger that reminds you of that person. I'll tell you the three people that remind me of Danny Hamilton, Joe Frank, Tommy Reynolds, and Alan Dennison.

We'll start with Danny Hamilton. It's a combination of the voice and looks of Engelbert Humperdinck that remind me of Dan. For Joe Frank, it's the personality and finesse of Michael Landon of TV's *Little House on the Prairie* that remind me of Joe Frank. As for Alan Dennison, it's the resemblance and personal character of Tom Hanks that reminds me of Alan. Tommy Reynolds I didn't get a chance to get to know well enough for that familiarity thing to evolve, but I can say that Tommy was a very gentle, spiritual human being, which you can hear in his music.

Point to Ponder

As a kid growing up, I collected baseball cards, and I remember thinking about how old the players looked. Now, at 57, as I'm getting up there in age myself, I look at today's baseball players and they seem so young. Once Humphrey Bogart starts to look young, I guess I'm going to have to admit I'm getting old!

Years after growing up, I went home and asked my mom about my baseball card collection, and she said, "Oh, son, I threw those out a long time ago."

Meeting a Real Superstar

While on tour with Hamilton, Joe Frank & Reynolds, we did a show in Hershey, Pennsylvania, that coincided with the bicentennial birthday of America. The group performed just across the street from the long stretch of steps that were in the mega-hit motion picture *Rocky* (1976). As famous as the Rocky statue itself are the stairs leading to the east entrance of the Philadelphia museum of art, also known as the Rocky Steps. We also got to tour the famous chocolate factory later on.

Somewhere around that time, we all got the opportunity to drive over by Yellow Cab to see the Carpenters in concert. Karen and Richard Carpenter were the members of one of the biggest brother and sister acts of the seventies. I remember all of us sitting in the audience to watch the show, which was quite an experience for me because all the shows I attended I spent working the stage, on the inside looking out.

The Carpenters did their show, and Karen played the drums, and when she stopped drumming to go front stage to sing, it was like an angel was before us. Her voice filled the concert hall, which I believe was an intimate outdoor venue. After the show, we all got up and walked down from our seats to the long line for the meet and greet. The group Hamilton, Joe Frank & Reynolds had, some years earlier, opened for the Carpenters at the infamous Hollywood Bowl. I had missed that show, and I was excited to meet the Carpenters for the first time.

The line moved quickly, and then there I was putting my hand out to meet Miss Karen Carpenter. As I shook her hand, I was startled by the fact that she was so frail and tiny in stature. I couldn't believe that the big, angelic voice that had belted out during the show came from this tiny person.

Later on, I heard that she passed away, on February 4, 1983, at the age of 33, from some kind of eating disorder. When I heard that, I remembered shaking her hand and getting the impression that she was frail.

The year H, JF&R played the Hollywood Bowl with the Carpenters, 1971, was the same year Hamilton, Joe Frank & Reynolds were nominated for that Grammy award for their song that went to #4 on Billboard's Hot 100, "Don't Pull Your Love (Out)."

I know that Danny was a smoker, but I wanted to know if it affected his singing as he belted out that song with such force. I remember asking Danny years later if he smoked cigarettes back when he sang that song.

Danny said, "No, not so much as now."

The Show of the World

A radio station in Los Angeles, KMPC, put on a show called *Show of the World* at the infamous Fabulous Forum, the venue where Jethro Tull (my brother Richard's favorite group) sold out six nights in a row in 20 minutes. Other artists performed there back in the day, including Three Dog Night.

The lineup from the KMPC *Show of the World*, from what I remember (and as I've said before, it's amazing what different things a group of people that experience a happening all at the same time take away from that experience), was Captain & Tennille; Foster Brooks; Liza Minnelli; and Hamilton, Joe Frank & Reynolds.

We had just come off a tour and did a one-off with the hilarious comedian Foster Brooks. That show was a charity concert in Bozeman, Montana, at Chet Huntley's Ranch, with Miss Donna Douglas, "Elly May" of *Beverly Hillbillies* and the lady that did the Serta mattress commercial, Joey Heatherton.

The morning after that show, everyone gathered in the dining area for breakfast. I sat right next to Miss Donna Douglas, which gave me an opportunity to tell Miss Douglas that my father really enjoyed her TV show. Across from me was June Lockhart of the TV shows *Lassie* and *Lost in Space*. Miss Lockhart even commented to me that she had also been a roadie at one time.

Alan Hale, Jr., "The Skipper" from *Gilligan's Island*, sat at the end of the long table. Since *Gilligan's Island* had been one my favorite shows when I was growing up, I couldn't resist getting up from the table when the ladies encouraged me, saying that they were sure he wouldn't mind. As nervous as I was, I actually got up and walked over and said hello.

"I just wanted to say that I really enjoyed the show you were on," I said.

He turned and smiled, and I headed back to my spot with the actresses June Lockhart and Miss Donna Douglas.

As I sat in the comfort of the lovely Miss Donna Douglas and mother figure June Lockhart, I couldn't help but think back just 48 hours to when I was driving the equipment truck alone cross country after the last show. I got pulled over by a cop on one of the back roads still far from Bozeman Montana's Chet Huntley's ranch, and the cop, upon reaching my window, pulled out his weapon, cocked the hammer back, and took my money, which was in an envelope with the gas receipts.

I was totally freaked out, all the while thinking, *I've got to get to the next gig on time and this cop is fucking with me.*

I didn't know what he was going to do next, but somehow, after all of that, he left. It was a very long time ago. I was about 23, with long hair, and I kind of remember sitting in the passenger seat of the suburban of our equipment truck with the cop sitting in the driver's seat.

I never told anyone about this. For years it would be a personal experience that haunted my memory. I planned to take it to the grave.

Later on, Joe Frank said to me, "Ronnie, get rid of those blank gas receipts."

Was Joe hinting to me that he'd noticed something unusual about the cash money versus the filled out gas receipts I had made? I was still too freaked out to tell Joe what had happened to me on those back roads of Montana. I'm as honest as the day is long, and anyone who knows me knows this, but being as young as I was I wanted to bury this experience, so I fudged the blank gas receipts to make up for what money the cop had taken from me at gunpoint!

I'd had the experience of having a gun in my face before when I was much younger and working alone at a fast food drive-through during the graveyard shift. A junkie walked up to the drive-through window, and I said, "Hello, what can I get you?"

Out came the gun pointed right at my face, and he motioned with the gun and pointed down to the safe. I reached down and rattled the safe handle to show him it was locked.

Still with the gun in my face, I said, "Look, there's some money in the register, and if you're hungry I'll make you something to eat."

I put the money in a bag, handed it to him, and bravely turned my back to him before I said, "Now, go! I'll give you a minute to get away."

I hoped that this would save my life, cringing and praying this shaky-looking junkie would not shoot me in the back or in the back of the head. As the seconds went by, I knew I could die at any moment.

Then the drive-through bell rang, indicating that a car was at the order menu and speaker.

The girl in the car said, "Hey, there's some guy trying to get over the back wall."

I was so relieved! I was happy I had escaped a fatal bullet to the head. I then called the police to report the incident.

But in Montana, after the cop left, I reached into my pocket and found just enough cash for gas to make it to Chet Huntley's ranch. I had to wait to eat until then. So when Miss Donna Douglas said to me, "Ronnie, you're a sweet fella," I felt absolution for all of the trauma and what had taken place. I still feel that Miss Douglas was, and is, as pure as an angel.

H, JF&R would smoke the Fabulous Forum show in Los Angeles, and it was the quickest 20 minutes ever! The sold out Fabulous Forum (now called the Great Western Forum, where the Lakers play basketball) was crowded with fans enjoying the high energy that was put out by the guys. What was especially awesome was that for this particular show, the artists that had played on the album were the ones on stage!

I still remember Joe Frank making a comment between songs that he felt like a yellow canary, referring to the bright yellow suit he was wearing. Then, after the next song, Joe Frank said, "Man, I feel like a baked potato up here" because of the bright lights of the stage.

I spent the concert hanging out with the man who was working the soundboard (which was about midway in the audience), making sure the sound came off well and supporting him by giving him cues when the solos were coming up in each song. If I had been a musician on that stage, I would have had to wear sunglasses because my eyes are very sensitive to those bright spotlights.

I would run into Captain & Tennille many years later in Lake Tahoe at a casino, and I had the chance to say hello. I can truly say that Toni Tennille was one of the most strikingly beautiful women I have ever met in my entire life, and her beauty is magnified when she sings.

One celebrity I wish I could have met is Marilyn Monroe. I was too young to know who she was growing up, but as we all do when we get older, we tend to like the stars of the past, whether on TV or from the music we heard when we were young. I have a short list of actresses I liked as a young man that I never got to meet, and one was Jane Greer. Google her name and you'll see what I mean. She was a lovely lady for sure. Another was Elizabeth Montgomery.

There were some stars I loved and never met, but once grown, I was lucky to serendipitously meet some of the stars that I heard and saw while growing up. There was one thing that I never got to do during the era of H, JF&R however, and that was to meet one of the stars my little sister Donna cherished and admired, Marie Osmond, of the famous TV variety show *Donnie & Marie*. Had I ever run into Marie, I would have asked her, as a favor to me, to phone my little sister and say "Hi, this is Marie Osmond. I'm with your brother right now, and he says that you are a big fan." But that never happened. I wanted so much for my sister to experience the same intense joy that hundreds of other kids did when I would bring them backstage for an autograph after shows all across the country to meet the group Hamilton, Joe Frank & Reynolds.

Kendon Studios, Burbank, CA

In the year of 1976 we all arrived at the recording studio in Burbank, CA, called Kendon Studios. The guys were booked for an early time slot, around 7 pm, so we arrived about 15 minutes early. The studio was ours until the wee hours because no one else had booked time for the rest of the day. We hung around outside of the recording part of the studio, where they had ping pong tables and other distractions to pass the time while we waited.

An hour and a half passed. It was now about 8:30 pm, and the artist was now into our slotted time for recording.

Finally, the artist came out, looking as if he just ran the New York marathon. It was Neil Diamond, trying to get the last part of his future hit song "If You Know What I Mean (Babe)," which hit #11 in 1976. He looked totally drained. I noticed his long, sweat-soaked, stringy hair hanging down past his shoulders as he came out with his arm around a girl who, I believe, worked at the front desk. She almost seemed to be helping him along, and they walked right by me, Danny, Joe, and Alan as we went into the same studio he had just left.

The remnants of a big bowl of fresh strawberries, grapes, and other fruit were still on the end console of the 48-channel mixing board. Days later, I was driving in my car and "If You Know What I Mean (Babe)" by Neil Diamond came on the radio, and I thought about how hard he had worked to get it right, keeping H, JF&D waiting while he mastered the ending to what I always thought was a great record, one that made it into my top 40 songs of all time. There was another one of his hits I liked of his a few years later called "Forever in Blue Jeans" (#20 in 1979).

In the recording studio that evening, as the engineer threaded the master tape and got things ready, he showed me how to clean the heads of the tape machine. One of the guest artists who had been hired to lay down some tracks arrived soon after. He shook everyone's hand, then got ready to do his "thing" on the guitar. He introduced himself as Jeff "Skunk" Baxter from the super group The Doobie Brothers. He had also played with another group called Steely Dan. You can hear his distinct guitar solo on the song "Reelin' In the Years" (#11, 1973), as well as in "Do It Again" (#6, 1972) and everyone's favorite, "Rickie Don't Lose That Number" (#4, 1974). Back then, Michael McDonald was part of the Steely Dan group as well.

So Jeff Baxter got his guitar out, and the engineer plugged him in "direct" in the control room as Jeff sat on a tall, bar stool-type chair and jammed away at a take. After a while, I left to run some errands, and when I returned about 5 hours later, Jeff was still in the chair working the solo that would be on the album *Love & Conversation*.

The guys took a break, and Jeff and Danny and Joe Frank were hanging out in the control room while Jeff told some stories. Jeff Baxter was not only an incredible guitar player; he was an outgoing and personable kind of guy as well. As we were chatting, he offered, "Yeah, if you guys want to go on the Doobie plane sometime . . ."

Just before the session started again, Jeff told the guys that he had handmade the very guitar he was playing for the current tracks of the H, JF&R/D album. The guys were simply amazed that he had carved the guitar out of his own coffee table. I really thought that this master of the guitar was great on all those songs I heard over the years, but there he was in person, laying down tracks for the group I worked for. If you get a chance, buy the album *Love and Conversation* and enjoy the songs that were recorded at Kendon Studios in Burbank, California.

[Authors note: Neil Diamond was paid $1,000,000 to perform at the Stockton Arena on January 15th, 2006, which is operated by their city, about a 30 minute drive south of Sacramento, CA. It got national attention and the city later fired that city manager for his actions, but it surely put the Stockton Arena on the map and put $1,000,000 in the pocket of Neil Diamond.]

Groucho Marx

I was just off the road after a tour and was on my way to Century City, where the business office was for H, JF&R, to pick up my check for working on the road, when I had one of those unexpected things in life happen that one has any idea is getting ready to occur.

While they were back-filing for my paycheck, one of the secretaries said to me, "Ronnie, would you like to meet Groucho Marx?"

I said, "Oh, jeez, I don't want to bother him."

She said, "Not a problem! He would love to meet you."

So my check arrived, and as I was turning to leave, the secretary said, "Ronnie, this is Groucho Marx. Groucho, this is Ronnie. He's with the group Hamilton, Joe Frank & Reynolds."

I shook his hand and remembered seeing him on those late night movies on TV. A very nice man he was, for sure. This was a great memory for me. The year was 1975, when Hamilton, Joe Frank & Reynolds had the # 1 hit song in the country, "Fallin' in Love." Life was very good then, and nothing compares to the heights of the year of 1975.

The Dry Cleaners

It's been a Hollywood tradition that the businesses in town, like dry cleaners and the Derby Restaurant, for example, post stars' pictures on their wall to support the community, but Danny would not have any part of it. I remember one time Danny Hamilton got really pissed off when he walked into the dry cleaners one day to pick up his clothes and saw his picture up on the wall. I had posted it, as there were some others of Hollywood star customers up from over the years. I don't remember if I took it down or not; it was a long time ago. It's possible that I went back to the cleaners and asked the owner to remove the 8x10 black and white picture of the group.

When Danny and I were out eating, people rarely came up to the coffee shop table to ask for an autograph, even after he'd been on *The Merv Griffin Show*, *The Diana Shore Show*, *Solid Gold*, *The Mike Douglas Show* and *Dick Clark's American Bandstand*. I'm sure Danny would have signed for a fan, but I think he just didn't get recognized. Maybe doing these television shows for just a few minutes while performing a hit kept them under the radar.

I remember when the group worked for a television studio in Hollywood, a program called *The Diana Shore Show*. I was down the hall, coming out of the green room, and as I was walking down the hall to the TV studio stage area, Charlton Heston walked by me. I said hello, and he said hello back to me as we walked past each other. Then, later during the taping, I was walking down the hall back to the stage and Charlton Heston was coming toward me again.

I said, "Hi."

Charlton Heston said, "I've already said hello."

I don't know why he said it that way or said that phrase at all, but there again is one of those "things" that memory retains for the later years to ponder.

The Union

Without warning, I can suddenly hear things my stepfather said over the years that have stayed with me and that come to mind, especially around Father's Day. Things like "Anything worth doing is worth doing right." Another one that is like a fine thread woven into my psyche is "Two wrongs don't make a right." The voice of my grandfather on my mother's side also comes to mind, and one of the things I hear him lamenting is "The unions, Ronnie, the unions!" Grandpa was from Palermo Italy.

I got to experience firsthand what the unions were about in television. In 1975, H, JF&R had arrived at the Merv Griffin studios in Hollywood to promote their current hit. I went into the stage area where Merv Griffin would eventually be taping and found the artists' stage where Danny and the guys would perform "Fallin' in Love." I had finished setting up, and as it got close to taping, the camera crew and television stage crew were arriving.

I always liked to step back and look over everything to see how it looked from the audience, then go up on stage and adjust the microphones for the singers, Danny, Joe, and Alan. But I only got one foot back on the stage when I heard, "STOP!" You know, like a cop would say. It kinda freaked me out.

The floor director came up to me and said, "You can't go up there now. The union won't allow it."

I thought, *Shit. What the fuck is this crap?*

He went on. "We'll go up and adjust the mics for you. Only the local television crew can work the stage area because it's a unionized area."

I said, "But what about the guitars for Joe Frank and Danny?"

The floor director said, "We'll have one of our people put the guitars up on the guitar stand."

I thought to myself, *There is no friggin way in hell anyone is going to touch the guitars.* So I went into the green room and told Dan what was up.

Dan said, "Ronnie, we'll just carry our guitars out."

Super Trouper

Hamilton, Joe Frank & Reynolds were touring on the road again. This time, it was a short tour about two weeks along the southern route of Texas-Alabama-Oklahoma. The group had just released "Light Up the World with Sunshine" (1976) which coincided with the build-up for America's bi-centennial birthday. Another great song from the guys. We came into a small town for a show that night and the group went to the hotel to rest up while I went straight to the venue. When I arrived at the venue, I was told by the promoter that there was no piano.

Of course, I thought to myself that Alan Dennison (Alan would always explain how to spell his name "like the chili") needed a piano to perform that evening. I thought for a moment and then asked some people where the closest church was.

We headed over, and I talked with the preacher and told him the situation. This was just after the tour when the song "Fallin' in Love" was #1 on *Casey Kasem's American Top 40 Countdown,* which may have helped in convincing the preacher to lend me the church piano for a donation from the group. The song was loved by all ages and was still heavily played on the radio.

The piano was delivered before the band was summoned from the hotel for the sound check. They arrived, walked out, and took their positions on stage, never having a clue of the scramble that had taken place hours before. After the show, Alan asked me to go out to the piano and get his ring, which he had left. When I got to the piano, I noticed blood on the keys from his incredible performance.

I remember the moment when I found out they'd put on the cover of the current album, *Love & Conversation,* "Ronnie 'Our Super Trouper.'" They must have figured out that title for me; I must have done some things they did find out about.

Another time, when the group was performing on stage in front of a crowd of thousands, Danny Hamilton stopped after a song and called me out because his amp had blown! I went out and checked the Fender amp to make sure it was not on standby or powered off. I then walked up to the lead microphone where Danny was standing, waiting to get an update on the situation, and at that moment—for a second or maybe two—I not only felt the energy from the crowd (like cannon fire, but in a good way), but I looked out past Dan to see thousands and thousands of fans waiting for the good news.

Then Dan leaned over to me and said "Ronnie, go by the amp and feel around the back."

As I did, Dan was facing me with his back to the audience, and he strummed his Fender guitar and there was sound!

Dan walked up to the lead microphone as the crowd applauded and cheered and said, "That's Ronnie, our Super Trouper, ladies and gentlemen."

At All Cost

A few hours after a show one night, Danny Hamilton was up in his room, and he phoned my room and said he was hungry and that the hotel restaurant had already closed. So I went up to his room and knocked on his door.

He said, "Can you take a cab into town and get me something to eat?"

I thought, *It's two in the morning. What's open?*

I said, "Sure!"

He gave me enough money for a cab ride, the equivalent of today's $300.00, and I was off. The cab took me about 30 miles from the hotel, but the nearest place was open and it was a diner!

When I entered the diner, the waitress knew right from the get-go because of my long hair that I must be with the concert that had performed hours before. It was always amazing to me how being part of the momentum of a tour carried an energy that people could see without even a word said to them about who you are.

I ordered the food and told the waitress that I was about 30 minutes from the hotel.

"Can you make it so the food will be hot when I get back to the hotel?" I asked. She agreed to try and even gave me real silverware! I paid for the food, left a tip, and got back in the cab. I arrived back at the hotel and paid for the cab driver what I owed, then tipped him on top of that because I knew if it was not for the cab, I would not have been able "at all cost" to get the request done for Danny. I know that after a show the musicians are so keyed up from the energy of the concert and tens of thousands of people that it takes a while for them to wind down and that when they do, the human body wants something to eat.

Stars in the Sky

If the group was on the tour bus, then I was on the bus. If they flew, I flew, with a few exceptions. We did a lot of flying. If we were not on the tour bus, we were in the air. One thing is for sure when traveling as much as we did: You see some Hollywood stars flying from here to there doing their promotional tours or going to and from gigs and shows. There was this one time the seating arrangement on the airplane had me serendipitously sitting next to a lady that I had just seen in a TV commercial.

Once the plane got in the air and the seat belt sign turned off, I looked to my right, as she was sitting near the window seat, and said, "Aren't you the lady on the commercial that's cleaning the oven? And you turn towards the camera and say, 'Sure, sure'?" (I guess the announcer was saying cleaning was easy or something.)

She replied with a big smile. "Yes! I'm Charlotte Rae."

I introduced myself, and we talked through the flight. My memory of Miss Rae from 1975 is a pleasant one. This was before her TV series *The Facts of Life* (1979). All the stars from Hollywood that I was fortunate enough to meet over the years were always smiling, always courteous, and always in a good mood.

Number 1 with a Bullitt (1975)

There was a time when the group actually got a limo ride from the airport, and I remember looking out the window thinking, *Wow, "Fallin' in Love" jumped to #1 on the Billboard's Hot 100 chart.*

Speaking of billboards, you could drive down Sunset Boulevard in Hollywood, pass the Playboy building, and as you were coming up on the infamous Tower Record Store, if you looked slightly up to your right, there was a replica picture of the "Fallin' in Love" album cover blown up and placed on one of the towering billboards that was larger than life.

Even while enjoying the thought of our success, I knew that someday this would all be over and I would be working a dreaded day job back in Los Angeles, so I tried to enjoy every moment. The group was dead set on treating the public respectfully and keeping our egos in check. The radio DJs and their staff treated us like kings, showing us the way to and from the hotel to the venue even in snowbound conditions.

No matter the treatment, the group would put on another show just like last night's show, which had been in a different city hundreds of miles away. The music set was pretty much the same every night. Joe Frank would write it out and I would go out on stage and tape the song list near each artist's amp, putting a copy up for the drummer as well. It was really the people and the fresh faces that kept things energized.

An artist that sells one million copies of a 45 rpm receives a gold record. HJF&R accomplished this and placed the record on their wall of shame at home with their other awards and pictures. By the way, selling 500,000 copies of an album 331/3 rpm (revolutions per minute when the vinyl was on the turntable and the needle played the song—remember those days?) receives a gold album. One million sold albums receives platinum. All these achievements were hard to accomplish back in the 70s, but H, JF&R got their gold!

One-Night Stands—Girls, Girls, Girls

Being in a different city every night and working for a famous group, especially while having a #1 hit on the charts, took a toll on me even years later. We were like magnets coming into town.

If we were not flying, we were driving. If we were driving, we would have the radio on as we came into the town we were going to work that night. Sure enough, as soon as we crossed the city limits, the DJ was talking it up about H, JF&R performing that night. Then he kicked out the #1 hit "Fallin' in Love," and everyone got excited as the energy went from normal to 1000 on a 1 to 10 scale.

This little welcome gave all of us a clear view of what was to be expected, because we all knew we were not the only ones listening to the radio. It's hard to decide whether our energy came from the air around the city or if it was generated from the experience of the previous show. You'd want to bottle the feeling and sell it, but the energy was only there for the moment we were in it and belonged to the event.

This, for me, made it difficult to adjust to regular life after the celebrity lifestyle of always being told we were great by the fans. The adulation people felt because of the music they listened to on the radio and the money they spent on the artists' music created a loyalty that was only intensified by actually being there in person with their favorite musicians.

Right after a show, girls would always gather around the stage to meet the guys in the group. I knew this because it was the same after every single show. There was a surplus of fresh faces and women wanting to stay the night. I would notice one girl after the show; that was the first stage. The second stage came later, when we arrived at the hotel and the girls would be waiting in the hotel lobby. The girl whom I had noticed was there in the lobby, sitting and waiting. There was this vibe, the kind you get when you know a woman is looking at you and wants you. There is no mistake, no thinking, *Is she looking at me?*

There were a few more women looking in my direction, and I knew I could pick out any one—or two—and I did. This became a habit for me, choosing, and later in life it was difficult for me when the girls at home expected a guy to approach them and not the other way around. Years of working this courtship, of me picking and choosing, would take its toll later in my life when there was no hit record and no H, JF&R to bring the ladies out of their hiding in droves to a public arena for entertainment.

I did get a little idea of how the ladies at home feel when they get approached a lot and after a while have to say "Don't bother me" or something like that and watch the guy take it to heart and walk away rejected. I only understood this after being approached every night, but I must admit that I liked it. I only wish the girls at home would do this approach thing. Carrying a backstage pass around my neck at home just would not cut it.

There were times after a show when the fans were ecstatic, nearly frenzied. They gathered by the dressing room door, and as I stood with them, I said "Okay, let's have a few of you for now and I'll be back for a few more until the group comes out."

So a few of the girls followed me through the door and down the hall to the dressing room, and Joe Frank yelled out before we got in, "Goddamn it, Ronnie, I'm not quite dressed yet!"

He was just pulling up his jeans. Anyway, the girls got their autographs and went away happy. This happened every night. The happiness, I mean, not the girls catching Joe dressing.

Seeing the fans really, really ecstatic with big smiles was a sight to remember, and I treasured bringing it about for them by being the one to pick out those that would want an autograph and to meet the group. Without sounding like a credit card commercial . . . when you bring happiness to another person, it's priceless!

Cruisin' Hollywood

Even after the group had broken up, Danny and I, still living in the Sherman Oaks area, would often hop in the car and go cruise Hollywood. As time went along, the two of us somehow ended up working on his music as a solo artist, which allowed us to hang out together and to do things together musically. I became like an unofficial personal road manager.

One day when I was visiting him, we decided to head down to Hollywood's Sunset Strip, where some of his friends were playing at the Whiskey A Go Go. We got into his car and headed out of his driveway towards the infamous Laurel Canyon, which at the end lets out into Hollywood. As we were headed in that direction, all of a sudden his #1 song, "Fallin' in Love" came on the radio.

I said, "Hey, wow, your song is on the radio and I'm here with you right now and we're getting ready to cruise the Hollywood strip." Danny looked at me and nodded his head with a smile. We were becoming close friends. While the group was formed and performing on tour, there was very little time for socializing. Yes, we all were together, but it was because of the job at hand. Now Dan was out of that scenario of a three-piece group known to millions, and he was evolving as a solo artist and I was right there and remained. As for Joe Frank and Alan, they had moved "out" of the music business.

As long as there has been a Los Angeles rock scene, there has been the Whisky A Go Go. An anchor on the Sunset Strip since it's opening in 1964, the Whisky A Go Go has played host to rock and roll's most important bands, from the Doors, Janis Joplin, and Led Zeppelin to today's up and coming new artists.

We were heading in that direction, and along the way, Danny told me that some years ago, when he was in his teens, he played guitar for a group called the Ventures, and that's whom we were going to see. He said that he also

pizza place and we heard in the background a jukebox playing Lionel Richie's #1 1984 hit "Hello." during the guitar solo in the middle of the song, I asked Dan if he'd done that session with Lionel Richie.

Danny said, "No, I wasn't in on that session."

I told him that the guitar solo in that song sounded like his playing.

Dan told me one time while we were at my father's duplex, recording some more songs with those guitars he had left, that he could tell when I was getting into the groove of a song and whether or not I thought it was a hit. I asked him how he could know this and he said, "Because your foot starts to move."

While the tape was rewinding back to the beginning, which gave us a few minutes of downtime, I asked him, "Where is this music you're creating coming from?"

He told me that when he writes a song he has Joe Frank in his mind for the bass guitar and Joe's sound. Then he has in mind while creating the music Alan on the baby grand piano and the way Alan sounded and so on.

I was intrigued by the whole concept, as I was a witness to the way a musician brings to life a new song. My observation up close was that Dan was tapping into something cosmic, the Universe.

I know there is something distinct going on with my voice, as people have mentioned it over the years. Elvis, I'm sure, could not hear what his voice was like. The reactions of others that listened to his records are all he could experience. When you listen to "Are You Lonesome Tonight" or his other ballad "Memories," it's bone-chilling, but Elvis could not experience his own voice. I never ever, ever, ever pointed out to Danny a comparison artist that sounded close to him. I left that alone. Danny Hamilton was becoming one of my best friends.

I hooked up with a truck driver about a month after my brother Richard passed away and did nothing but travel the United States and Canada for a while. C.W. McCall had a #1 hit out in late 1975 that got a lot of airplay, and by the time I hit the road trucking around late 1977, it was a big fad and the CB craze hit the air waves as well. I needed to be moving again.

Once a roadie always a roadie

18 Wheels on the Road

About a month after my brother died on September 7, 1977, while living in one of my father's owned duplexes, I met a truck driver who hauled furniture for one of the top four movers in the USA for all 50 states and Canada, Atlas Van Lines.

I was still missing my brother and dealing with all the things that come with a tragedy in the family, especially when it's suicide. Like Jim Morrison of the Doors and other artists in their 20s that died suddenly, my brother was only 26 years old when he checked out, and life for him had still seemed full of promise. I didn't know how long this dark cloud would hang over me. I found out through future experiences that it would take at least four seasons to get to a level where I could be out of the slump. I was only 23 years old, soon to be 24 on December 2.

I heard someone say one time that anybody, stranger or not, deserves help when they're walking into trouble. The true Sagittarius that I am was always looking out for others. Unbeknownst to me, an opportunity was coming my way, brought by fate when I was at a coffee shop.

I was taking a break from the quadruplex where I was living with all of Danny's guitars, amps, and recording things that were waiting to be used when he came to visit. The trucker that I would soon help out of a dilemma was Roger, a professional driver out of Ohio. Roger had been state champion for 7 years in a row in a weightlifting class called the clean and jerk. Roger looked like the actor Lou Ferrigno of the TV show *The Incredible Hulk*, whom, incidentally, I got to meet and shake hands with years earlier while he was filming in a segment of a future broadcast in Hollywood.

I was dating Lou Ferrigno's hair dresser at the time. She would prep his hair between takes, and during one of the longer breaks, she said to me, "Ronnie, would you like to meet Louie?"

I said, "Sure!"

So we went over to the area where Lou Ferrigno was waiting for his next cue and I was introduced. We shook hands, and later I looked at my hand and saw that the green they used for coloring his skin had rubbed off onto my hand. Many years later, I would meet Lou Ferrigno again at one of his live appearances at a famous gym in Sacramento, California. When I went up to him and shook his hand the second time, there was no green paint, but he said he remembered me from years ago when he was filming TV's *The Incredible Hulk*.

At the coffee shop, Roger was on the payphone (this was before cell phones, remember?) and I was at the counter having a cup of coffee when fate stepped in. Roger had been talking loudly enough for me to hear that he was having a tough time with whatever it was he was dealing with. So when he hung up the phone, I asked if I could help out.

He said "Well, I'm just passing through, and last night they towed my truck and I need to go to the yard to get it out of impound."

So I gave Roger a ride over to the yard, and along the way he told me what had happened. As with a lot of line drivers, truckers coming into town the night before they had to unload a shipment would get near the unloading site and stay the night in the sleeper of their 18-wheeler until morning. Roger had parked at the Santa Anita Mall parking lot near the Santa Anita race track. I knew this area as I had worked as a teenager at the Santa Anita shopping mall.

Roger continued his story, telling me that while he was asleep in his rig, the cops showed up and started banging on his driver's door. That did not go over well with Roger. He felt that he was not bothering anyone, not to mention that he was parked too far out of the way for anyone to be concerned about taking a few parking spaces in an area of the parking lot where nobody parked anyway, especially this late at night.

When Roger woke up to the pounding on his driver's door, he just got behind the wheel, cranked up the big rig, and started to move slowly forward, then eventually in a circle. This went on for a few minutes with the cop car following behind, lights flashing and bullhorn telling Roger to pull over and get out!

He stopped the rig, got out, and I'm sure the cop's face had a look of surprise as the 6-foot 3-inch state champion weightlifter stepped down from the 18-wheeler. This is everyone's reaction when they first see Roger. The police arrested him without incident and then took him in, but he was released the next day, and that's why I met Roger in the coffee shop.

Just think; if Roger didn't get arrested I never, ever would have met him. Yes, hind sight truly is 20/20.

After Roger finished the paperwork and was ready to get his rig out of the impound yard, I told Roger that he was welcome to come by the apartment and shower and have some coffee. It was years ago, but I think I was already thinking about the possibility of going back on the road, this time trucking across the country in a big rig!

As Roger and I were talking about what I was doing and what had happened just a month earlier with my brother's death, I realized that I was up for keeping myself in motion. Staying at my apartment did not appeal to me; this kept me feeling stagnant. I wanted to be on the move, and Roger's way of life traveling across the country, moving people and all their furniture and personal belongings from state to state, seemed to be the right kind of medicine I needed at that moment in time.

I was just 24, healthy, and I didn't know a 10-speed from a 13-speed gearshift, but I was ready to see the country. So I jokingly said to Roger, "What time we pulling out?"

He said, "Ronnie, if you really want to go on the road, we head out at seven sharp."

I was ready at 7 am with a suitcase and shaving kit; anything else I needed I could buy at a truck stop store. We headed out early, and the rig was started up and I got in on the passenger side and we were rollin'!

As I was studying Roger as he shifted the gears of the big rig, he gave me the 4-1-1 on what would be going on for the next 24 hours. There was a stop in Arizona where I could call my dad to tell him to call Danny Hamilton and make sure he got his guitars out of the apartment and put my personal stuff in storage. Since my dad owned the quadruplex and lived in the other quadruplex across the way, I was confident that Danny would get the message and my dad would let him in to get his instruments.

We were southbound and down! It was great to be on the move again. It was not a music tour, but I made sure that along the way we were able to hook up with some of my connections and get backstage passes to some of the concerts that were going on in a city we happened to be in if there was a concert.

As we approached New Orleans, Louisiana, where the Doobie Brothers were opening for the Rolling Stones, we rolled into town about the same time they were performing at the Superdome. I told Roger how we would work getting close to the artists by pulling around the backstage area of the venue. I would handle it from there.

We pulled up to the Superdome backstage area in the big rig. I got out and walked up to the wooden fence that had a knot hole the size of a silver dollar. I talked to someone through that knot hole and asked for the guitarist for the Doobie Brothers, and they ran down Jeff 'Skunk" Baxter, who you may remember had done some guitar work in the studio for H, JF&R/D a couple years earlier. Jeff came to the fence and put his index finger through the hole and said, "Hey, Ronnie, good to see you. What brings you to New Orleans?"

I said, "Jeff, I'm just passing through. I'm trucking for a while. Could you get me and a buddy in to see the show?"

Jeff said, "Hang on, Ronnie. I'll be right back!"

He came back a few minutes later to tell me that security was tight because he was opening for the Rolling Stones. There weren't even t-shirts that said SECURITY on them—which, if there had been, would have allowed Roger and I to get in backstage and hang out with Jeff and his band mates before and after the show. But there was no chance for that to happen because security was airtight for the greatest rock and roll band in the world, Mick Jagger and the Rolling Stones.

I said "No problem, Jeff. I'll talk to you down the road when I get back to California."

Then Roger and I were off again to another state.

We did get to see a concert and hang out at the Hotel Holiday Inn party with Boz Scaggs a few months later. About a year later, we were in Colorado where jazz artist Al Jareau was playing. Since Al Jareau had hired the studio drummer from H, JF&R, we got some primo seats.

Roger asked, "So, Ronnie, you set up Joe Junior's drums?"

I replied, "Oh, yeah!" I mentioned to Roger that no matter how many times you set up for a drummer or how many years you work for that drummer, he still will come out during the sound check to sit on the drum stool and adjust the drum kit as if it were a glove he was putting on. I also said that there was a drummer, not the one we're getting ready to meet, but that he was so picky that he would take all the cymbals off just after the show and pack them into a sleeve and carry them off, leaving the rest of the drum kit for me to take down. He just did not want anyone to touch his drums, as he said before he was hired on to tour with H, JF&R. But after he watched me work the stage, he came up to me and said, "Ronnie, I see that you really care for and have pride in what you are doing. Go ahead and set up my drums from now on, but I will always take the cymbals in my carry-on case on the plane."

After the show, I was able to treat Roger to backstage and to meeting Joe Carerro, Jr., who had played on every album H, JF&R recorded.

I said, "Joe Junior, this is a good friend of mine, The Incredible Hulk! Just kidding; it's Roger. And Roger, this is Joe Junior."

Roger said to Joe, "It's a pleasure to meet you. Ronnie talks about Hamilton, Joe Frank & Reynolds all the time."

Joe Jr. (who was also a cousin to Joe Frank) was a gracious host to us, coming into town off the cuff like we did. He really treated us well.

Then we were off again, heading to another state. I think we even had, playing on the stereo, that song of Ole Willie Nelson's, "On the Road Again." We were still trucking at about the same time as the TV show *BJ & The Bear*, (1978) which we would comment on as we saw on the road the same type of big rig the star of the TV show, BJ, was driving, the state-of-the-art Aerodyne made by Kenworth. The Aerodyne was, at that time, the very fanciest of rigs, with all the bells and whistles.

We eventually were in every state and even in Canada. The border of USA and Canada was very loose back in those days. You didn't even need a passport, just a driver's license. When we had a load of furniture going into Canada from the United States, the guards at the border crossing were very polite. I remember still to this day the way the folks of Canada would greet you with a "Nice day today, eh?"

The border guards would have us stop so they could seal the truck, and then that seal could not be broken for any reason until we arrived at our destination according to our paperwork. Once we arrived at our destination, the seal would be broken by the people in charge and then we could unload the shipment.

Sometime during my trekking with Roger, we stopped at Roger's home town of Akron, Ohio, and got to see a live Pro football game at the stadium, Cincinnati versus Philadelphia. Just before hitting the road again, a friend of his suggested that I go see this psychic. I thought it would be cool. The psychic gave me a reading and I wrote down what I could as she gave it. Psychic Jan Nash mentioned some things that, years later, came to pass. I lost those notes trucking around the country, but I remember a little of what she said.

"Ronnie, something to do with your voice, like singing." She continued, "You don't want to be bouncing around in a truck the rest of your life."

I also remember her saying that there was a girl, and her initials were LB (she even said the words "as in pound"), and she commented that this girl was very changeable. This would be Leah, whom I would meet 5 years from then. And yes, her initials were LB.

Jan also said, "You will also meet Joe Walsh of the group the James Gang." Those were her very words. Jan said she did a reading for him as well and asked that when I met him I would tell him that Jan Nash says hello. The things I remember and mention here have come to pass, except the meeting of Joe Walsh, now guitarist for the super group The Eagles.

I learned how to drive the 18-wheeler. It was a Chevy Titan 90 Cab-over that Roger was using to run all 48 states and Canada. I took the written test and driving test, passed, received my Class 1 license, and kept it for many years even though trucking would not be my career later in life. I would drive at night and Roger drove during the day while I slept in the sleeper. There were a lot of things one sees out on the road, but I'll just mention this one time that I was driving.

It was early morning and the sun was just coming up. Once in a while, a trucker would drive by and say "Good morning there, 18-wheeler" and I would pick up the CB radio and say, "Morning."

So I'm driving along, and as I'm coming up around the curve of this two-lane road cutting through town, I saw a huge oak tree that was over a hundred years old, big and wide. As I was making the curve, I saw that another big rig had plowed directly into the tree and the cab of his 18-wheeler was wrapped around the entire tree. He'd hit hard, and as I was coming out of the turn I thought to myself, *He must have fallen asleep while driving.*

Yes, it's dangerous out there on the road, and as I was thinking about that big rig wrapped around the oak tree, I remembered how Roger (who was sleeping in the sleeper) told me the very first time I got the hang of driving, "Ronnie, don't try to be a big man and drive all night. As soon as you start to get tired, pull over and I'll take it from there. Truck driving is hard work, and I had to work up a little at a time to make it up to an eight-hour shift. Like working out in the gym, you build up to it a little at a time."

I had a lot of respect for Roger, who had an incredible recall (like Jackie Gleason). His major in college had been History, and he'd played college football as well. We would pass the time on the road sometimes by listing the capitols of each state, that kind of thing. He knew it all, even the detours across the country. He was also a fan of the big ships from the renaissance era that sailed the 7 seas. I thought many, many times that Roger would definitely be our bus driver should Hamilton, Joe Frank & Reynolds get together again and tour. I knew the musicians could go to sleep on the tour bus and we all would be safe. No one would fuck with us either because of Roger's presence.

Once, we were at a truck stop somewhere down south, at a Truckstops of America I think, and it was one of the busy ones. We finished up breakfast and were standing in line at the cashier to pay. Finally, when Roger stepped up, the local girl that was employed at the truck stop looked at Roger in his tank top and said as she was handing him back his change, "You are deserving of that shirt."

The ladies were drawn to Roger. He had that same magnetism that bass player Joe Frank had; it was something special. Roger was like a big brother to me, and I'll never ever forget him.

I've mentioned how memory works in strange ways for all of us on planet Earth. I remember one time while trucking the USA with Roger, we were in a truck stop having breakfast at the counter. For some reason, Roger had called home and was pissed off. He handled his anger in a very controlled and unique way. Back then, they had ashtrays on the tables and counters. Roger took out a hundred dollar bill and held a lit match to it. As it burned, he set it in an ashtray nearby.

I said, "Damn, Roger, that's a full tank of fuel."

The price of diesel fuel at the time was 32 cents a gallon.

The waitress came over and said, "That isn't a real 100 dollar bill, is it?"

Roger wordlessly took out a fifty dollar bill and set it on fire.

I told the waitress, "Shhh. Yes, it's real."

A preacher had a line that went something like: "Treat others right because what you do to others will come back to you." I wish Roger well, and God bless him for taking me under his wing for the nearly 3 years I spent with him out on the road.

I trucked from 1977 until sometime in 1979.I took a break from trucking and flew home to the great state of California from one of the Midwestern states when Roger decided to visit his family. I met up with Danny Hamilton, and we eventually got the infamous house in Burbank, California. But first, there were a few more mountains to climb.

Point to ponder

Being raised Catholic, I had read from the Bible and I always wondered if there really was a flood. I believed that Jesus did walk the earth even the Jews believe Jesus was here, but they don't believe he is the son of God. While trucking across the country with Roger, we came into a small town in the southwest Arizona area. The hotel we stayed at was an out-the-way place from the inner city, like out in the desert. You could walk outside in the middle of the night, lay down on one of the lawn chairs by the pool, and as you were looking up into the darken sky, you could see billions and billions of stars. Crystal clear was the evening sky. Since there were no bright lights on, in, or around the pool area, you were able to really see the stars so clear that they seemed so close you could reach out and touch one.

The following day, before we headed back onto the road to take a shipment to the east coast, I took a swim, and as I was laying out on one of the lawn chairs with some other folks that were staying at the hotel, I started talking with an older man, and he mentioned in his broken German accent that he was an archaeologist. My opportunity had arrived to ask, "Was there a flood?"

He simply stated, with his thick German accent, "Yes! The highest mountain in the world, 300 feet above that."

Gypsy Out of the Bottle

I don't remember where I was in Southern California or why I was there, but I needed money and I knew that truckers, when they arrived at a town truck stop, sometimes would look for workers to help unload for a flat fee or a percentage. Either way, it was good money and quick because the truck drivers would pay cash. Having a few bucks at the end of a hard day's work was satisfying, especially when you had to pay a past-due bill or used it to eat.

It was a constant hustle. I was not one to go through the doors of the welfare department and ask for help. There was a moment, and I mean a moment—like maybe 3 minutes—when I did go through the doors one time with a future girlfriend, but after pondering and looking around, I said to Leah, "Let's go. This is not for us." This 3-minute turnaround happened a few years after trucking with Roger when I eventually meet my first love, Leah. Had they had a revolving door, I would have used that. I could have been in and out much quicker.

I was now local on the west coast, and Roger was home somewhere on the east coast. I hooked up with a rogue trucker at a 76 truck stop, planning to do a short run from Los Angeles to Las Vegas and unload furniture. When done, I would take a Greyhound bus home. But when we were unloading in the outlining area of Vegas, the trucker copped an attitude as we were finishing up and refused to take me into the city to the Greyhound Station.

"Here's some money," he said. "Now walk back to Los Angeles!"

So there I was, walking, and it was closing in on evening. Luckily, I had on tennis shoes, and I walked and walked and walked for miles along the main road, trying to hitch a ride. Unfortunately, there was very little traffic. Sometimes I could even walk in the middle of the road to get a better view of what was ahead and behind. I was thankful that it was not raining, though I have walked long distances in the rain with lightning and thunder all around.

As I was walking, I thought back to when I walked for miles and miles as a kid in the Tujunga wash on the weekends. This, however, was not as fun. As I walked, I couldn't help but fall into thoughts about the current situation. All my experiences with black musicians were pleasant, but this black truck driver was no musician. The rig was his ship, and he had asked me to get off. There was no negotiating and I didn't argue the point; I just started to hoof it on down the road.

I knew without a doubt that I was a long way from home and that I was totally alone, and I was feeling that down and out feeling of boy, I surely could use a friend about now.

Years after, I did a walkathon for one of the radio stations I worked for early on in my radio career. The city roped off the streets for that 25-mile Sunday walk. For some reason, I was wearing dress shoes because I had no tennis shoes at the time, probably because I was low on funds. I got horrible blisters, and I stopped at about mile 13 and was driven in a golf cart to the finishing line where the cars were parked.

I think that even if I was filthy rich, I would still only have one pair of shoes. Well, maybe I would get a pair of tennis shoes too. Thinking about these rich folks that buy five or 10 cars that just sit around in the carport or garage . . . how is it that they have to have more than one, maybe two? I understand having a house on the east coast and another on the west coast— near the ocean, of course. If I ever do get the big bucks, I'll try to remember how thrifty I am now and have a bit of self control.

Anyway, after a lot of thinking to myself, no one had yet stopped to give me a lift into Vegas. I realized then that I would have to take care of myself. It's funny, thinking in this "rejected" frame of mind. I was thinking about when I was working for the local furniture-moving company in the Valley, near Hollywood, for extra money. I was asked to head over to the warehouse to let a customer in so he could go through the stuff he was storing.

It was Mickey Dolenz of the Monkees. He opened his storage unit and he had a shitload of t-shirts from a TV commercial he was doing at the time called Miller's Outpost.

He said, "Ronnie, I appreciate you opening up the unit. Here, take a box of shirts with you when you leave."

I even got to tell him about Hamilton, Joe Frank & Reynolds, which had long ago broken up. You just never know who, what, or where you will bump into in this old world.

I eventually did get a ride from someone that was heading into Vegas who kindly dropped me off at the Vegas truck stop. It was an exhausting lesson, but I learned not to head out with a truck driver just off the cuff. Maybe he just didn't like Italians. I'd learned to trust my instincts over the years, but it appeared that this truck driver was a stroke of bad luck for me, and after that the gypsy in me was back in the bottle—for a while, anyway.

I also learned over the years that people have issues and carry a lot of baggage!

It's been many years; I was still in my twenties, but I have this vague memory of loading up everything I owned and consciously planning to relocate from Los Angeles to Las Vegas to work the truck stops there and try to settle. I don't even remember what year it was, but I know it must have been just after I completed my time with Roger. Fate again would pull me back from straying off too far.

I had stopped in Victorville to stay in a hotel for the night before the final 200-mile stretch on Highway 15 to Vegas in the morning. The next morning, I woke up, got ready, and was thinking about what I would have for breakfast as I headed out the door of the Motel 6 to the parking lot.

My next thought was, *Where is my car?*

I looked and looked for a while, going through a frantic checklist of what I had done when I checked in the night before. This was no "Where did I leave my car keys?" The car was gone! Stolen!

I made a report with the local police and then decided to return home to Los Angeles. It was a long time ago, but I remember that the return journey was a struggle; I had very little money and I did a lot of walking through little towns trying to catch a ride back to Los Angeles. I even tried calling some close friends in Los Angeles when I passed a phone booth, but no one seemed available to answer their phone. There was no cell phones back then; answering machines weren't even commercially available. You may notice that a lot when watching an old movie, the way the actor is calling someone and the phone just keeps on ringing and you think to yourself, Hey, leave a message on the answering machine.

So I walked and walked, alone again and realizing that I had to, once again, take care of myself. There was no rescue this time, and it was another hard life lesson learned for sure. Looking back with, as they say, 20/20 hindsight, it appears to me that fate had some kind of play in stopping me dead in my tracks (as the expression goes). I had strayed too far. With all the cars parked in the hotel parking lot, the criminal had chosen mine.

According to the locals, that 200-mile strip from the hotel where I'd stayed to the city of Las Vegas is notorious for the frequency with which people take cars and joyride into Vegas. I look back on a lot of things over the years, and it sure seems to me that many things are destined just by the way some of the major, critical turning points in life have obvious signs of a touch of some kind of control or plan.

There have been a few times that, at the moment of something happening—because it happened with such precision and the accuracy of, say, the planets aligning perfectly or the sun coming up every day without a hitch—one is made to believe that God intervened. Why there are some things in life that are favored over others is a mystery. Generally, most all of our life experiences tend to keep us all on the right track.

Not long after I had finally made it back home to L.A., the highway patrol found my car abandoned at a rest stop just outside Vegas. We have all heard the sayings of mothers telling their kids to make sure they have clean underwear because you never know if you are going to be in an accident. I say, make sure you have a good pair of jogging shoes!

Pictures from the Past

Me (with my Jethro Tull hair) and Mom visiting my brother Richard and Connie's house

**Miss Donna Douglas (Elly May of the Beverly Hillbillies)
horseback riding in Bozeman Montana**

My brother Richard

From left to right: my niece Tina, my brother Richard, my niece Kristine, Connie, and my sister Donna

Danny Hamilton at His home relaxing

My niece Kristine and her family

Sue from the Burbank house 1979

Danny Hamilton and Alan Dennison at Alan's home, 100 yards from the Beach (3rd floor)

Sister Mary Bridgette Ann- leading us into Our Lady of Lourdes church - 1962 (receiving first Holy Communion)

Me at 5 years old arriving in Glendale, CA

Back yard patio of 10326 Pinyon Ave. Tujunga, CA w/my dog Fuzzy

MKB and his family; Cindy, their son Patrick, and MKB (James Cagney) Christmas – 1994 – I took the picture

**From left to right-Danny Hamilton, c: Joe Frank Carollo r;
Tommy Reynolds (photo courtesy of world renowned
photographer, Ed Caraeff)**

From left to right; Danny Hamilton lead vocals/guitar; c.
Joe Frank Carollo, bass/vocals r. Alan Dennison, Baby
Grand piano. (Photo courtesy of world renown
photographer Ed Caraeff)

My Brother Richard's first daughter Tina (1986)

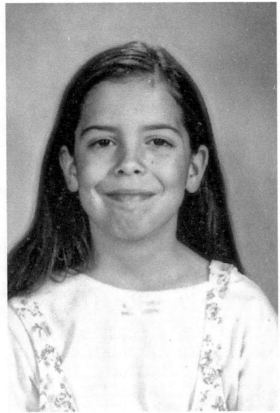

Misty, Connie's 3rd daughter

My kid sister Pam, the sassy Irish/Italian. r. Donna my other sister

Ross du Clair

Ronnie and Bob Malik "LIVE" remote at the Arden Fair mall (Sacramento, CA on COOL 101.1)

On tour w/Hamilton, Joe Frank & Reynolds of the amusement parks across the country. Just got off the roller coaster ride.

**Station manager Gerry Cagle of KWOD 106 Sacramento, CA
(photo courtesy of Gerry Cagle)**

**M G Kelly aka, Machine Gun Kelly # 1 jock at 93 KHJ Los
Angeles, CA (photo courtesy of MG Kelly)**

Ronnie on the balcony of Alan Dennison's 3rd floor apt.
100 yards from the ocean. Ronnie's studio apt on the bottom
floor.

Ronnie working the phones at 2 years old!

World renowned photographer Ed Caraeff had some film left in his camera while photographing Hamilton, Joe Frank & Reynolds next album.

Ronnie adjusting Danny Hamilton's vocal mic in Fresno California.

On the air at COOL 101

Ronnie, holding the final long term goal he set out, at the
very beginning of his radio career, which was; to achieve
[one of the] top 5 radio markets in the USA. (San Francisco,
CA, is radio market #4)

Ronnie as concert promoter stops for a moment to
take a picture, during the set-up of the world famous group,
America. Their signature mega hit; A Horse with no
name.

Duty calls

Voiceover in the Studio

Danny and I had serendipitously met the original engineer on the #1 hit "Fallin' in Love" coming out of a 7-11 store in Sherman Oaks, California. So when Danny Hamilton was working on his solo album, he had about four of the songs ready to use for shopping around town at all of the record companies in the Hollywood area. While the engineer and Danny and myself were all gathered in the control room, listening to the playback recording of the finishing touches done in the studio, Danny said, "Okay, Ronnie, go in the studio and stand at my vocal mic and introduce the four songs."

So I went in the studio and introduced the first song, "Cry in the Night."

Dan hit the talkback button on the console and said, "Wow, it's kinda like singing, huh, Ronnie?"

I really didn't think about that part of the inflection; I was just doing what came naturally and talking along the introduction of the music.

"Yes, I guess it is a little of that," I replied. Still years away from broadcasting school and actually being "on the air," I was doing what came natural while talking over the music. I had hung around radio stations before and practiced in their production studios, but that was the extent of my experience. I didn't know it then, but that was just another indicator of a hidden talent just waiting to emerge in good time. Jan Nash the psychic seemed to be right that I would be doing something with my voice, which would come to light in just a few years.

The Burbank House 1979

Fate is more than a feeling. Fate is something that makes things happen outside of our conscious intentions. I guess it is being guided, for lack of a better word.

I was just 26 years old and had been dating a waitress that worked at Twains Restaurant on Ventura Boulevard in Sherman Oaks, California, a place where Danny and I always liked to eat. Just down the street was the famous Baked Potato nightclub, where top jazz artists played through the smoke-filled room in an atmosphere that was laid back like in old black and white movies on television. Dan and I would hang out at the Baked Potato for quick drinks and to check out the musicians on a regular basis. Sometimes afterwards, we would walk up the street to 31 Flavors and get thick chocolate chip shakes, one of Dan's favorites, before walking home and talking along the way. Even to this day, I stop once in a while to get one of those shakes and think about the great times. Memories are great to have.

The waitress I was dating had a two-bedroom house with a large backyard and a Jacuzzi. She couldn't afford the house, so Danny took it over. I took one of the bedrooms, at Danny's invitation, and Sue, the waitress I was dating, moved on to other things. I liked Sue, and I still to this day have a picture of her. Sue was the kind of girl that would cook everyone a big breakfast, but when she started to get domestic on me, ironing my shirts and things like that, I had to say to her, "Whoa, wait a minute!" She really was a cool chick though.

Everyone enjoyed the barbecues that Danny and I held in the big backyard, which had a covered back porch and shade trees and, if I remember right, a gazebo. While we lived at the infamous Burbank house, Danny's future wife, Fredricka, often stopped by to visit him, as did his brother Judd and lots of other friends as well. It was a busy household.

One time, Danny said to me, while we were just hanging around the house, "Ronnie, I've been watching you, and you seem to make the right moves, the right decisions. It's like you're being guided."

I thought that since my brother had just been buried 22 months earlier, maybe it was my brother Richard. Another time, when I was doing the day job thing again, delivering around the Los Angeles metro area for one of the larger messenger service companies, I was dropping off a package at a corporation and a very pretty, intuitive secretary said out of the blue, "You have someone that is standing behind you. He's big and tall." She emphasized again that he was big, "an Indian spirit guide." At the time, I thought, *Wow, what a trip.* I didn't dwell on it too much, but I do remember her words clearly.

Danny took the time to critique the songs I wrote and helped me develop timing and an ear for where the rhyme would come into play during the verses. Some years later, I wrote about four songs and waited for an opportunity to show Danny what I was doing, hoping he could put some music to some of the lyrics and record them and see how it came out. Music is timeless until it is heard. But the songs that I wrote never got a chance to be recorded or seen by Danny. The right time and place to present what I wrote to him just slipped away.

Besides, I was really more into developing my radio skills and keeping up with the hits every Sunday morning. I listened religiously to a radio show called *Casey Kasem's American Top 40 Weekly Countdown.* I realized that I had a knack for picking a hit and predicting how far it would go on the American Top 40 Countdown. On occasion, I would even attempt a Record of the Year or Song of the Year prediction. Dan had told me early on that the Record of the Year award was for the performing artist or the production, producer, and engineer. Song of the Year was the artist that created the song.

Now, every song I heard was not a smash hit to me. There were many great songs and I enjoyed listening to them, but my internal gauge for smash hits was more of a cream of the crop type of thing. So, whether it was on the charts or just starting at the "entry position" on the Billboard Hot 100 charts, it didn't matter.

One thing was for sure, though: After hearing a song in the studio over and over, maybe 150 times, when I heard that same song playing on the radio it was instantly like hearing it for the first time. Aside from knowing at the very moment when the DJ kicked out the song title and artist that there were thousands of listeners hearing also, radio just gives a song a fresh, crisp sound. Sometimes, depending on the recording studio, the engineer would reach into his bag and pull out a transistor radio and say, "Okay, guys. Here is what it will sound like on the radio!"

There was a hit out a year earlier by Barry Manilow called "Can't Smile Without You" that was #3 in 1978, and I told Danny that listening to that song was depressing.

"It's like it's someone whining about something."

Danny said that he thought it was a "smart song" by Manilow, and that gave me another way of listening to it. For me, when it came to picking a hit, the song had to be uplifting, a feel-good thing that touched a nerve that told me it was a hit way before anyone knew it was or before it had entered the Hot 100. My foot just did not move to Barry Manilow's record. I remember I could actually be in a deep sleep and, if I left the radio on overnight, when an H, JF&R song came on, I would come out of even a deep sleep. Then, as I was wrestling myself awake, I could hear their song playing away. That's how deep into my being the love I had for this group was.

When things got tight for rent, we had to deal with the same landlord my friend Sue had had to deal with. Danny would tell me to sell one of his many guitars. I put an ad in the paper for the white Falcon gold inlay guitar and the road manager for the group Chicago stopped by and bought it.

There was this girl I met on the road that I'd kept in touch with and was starting to fall for—not hard, but just starting to fall. It was another form of puppy love, but an older version, a mid-20-year-old version. Around that same time, Peaches and Herb had a smash hit out called "Reunited," which was #1 (1979), and whenever I heard it played it connected me with her in my mind. When she sent me a Dear John letter from Utah, I was a little despondent, to say the least.

When Danny read the letter, he put his hand on my shoulder and said to me, "Ronnie, don't you worry. When we play the Salt Palace, that will show her!" His emphasis about the Salt Palace was that it was as grand as the Royal Albert Hall in London where the Beatles played.

Just then, the phone rang, and when Danny had answered it he said, "Ronnie, it's for you."

I walked up to the wall-mounted phone in the kitchen and said, "Yes, hello?"

And I was told by a family member that my natural father had just died. My dad, who brought me into this world, was now gone, and he had only lived to be 50 years old. I went over to the couch to sit down, and Danny put his arm around me and said, "Ronnie, I don't know why you have to go through so much at such an early age."

As I drove out of town alone for the funeral a few days later, I was thinking, *That's the second time my stepdad has called me to tell me there was a death in the family.* He did not say, "Your father has passed away;" he said my dad's name, John.

I was totally drained, and during the funeral at the cemetery, when I looked up, there was Danny Hamilton. I remembered, at that very moment after looking up, when I went to visit Danny in Hollywood and he left a note on his front door that he would be right back and he signed it "Your true friend." I was thinking about my father and how devastated he had been when, two years earlier but only a few yards away, he had cried over the grave of his firstborn, my big brother. I knew I had made the right decision in burying my father right next to my brother, though everyone had pulled me in many directions.

People always seem to come out of the woodwork on these occasions: relatives, cousins, in-laws, etc., but I was next in line for the power to decide where my father would be buried. My Aunt Minnie from New Jersey, my father's sister, insisted on sending him back east to be buried near where she lived. I knew that they were very close as brother and sister. My aunt Minnie would come out from Jersey to visit on occasion, and she genuinely showed love and affection toward us kids as well as her brother. Being only in my mid-20s, I thought, *Wow, I and only I have to make the decision about where my father will be buried.* My father was divorced from my mom, so I had to think about this all on my own.

I went into a back room because there were over 75 people in the house. I closed the door and sat in my father's chair and thought about things my dad had told me over the years, taking deep breaths, exhaling, trying to relax. Danny Hamilton had taught me some meditation techniques, and I applied the things I knew that would bring me to a relaxed state.

I thought about the time a while ago when Hamilton, Joe Frank & Reynolds put my name on their *Love and Conversation* album. I was so excited. I felt like I had just received an Academy Award. I drove about an hour from Hollywood, where I lived, to the very house I was sitting in and showed my father with enthusiasm that my name was on the album with the title "Our Super Trouper." My Sicilian father, being from the era of the Great Depression, said to me as he held the album, his hand slightly moving, "When are you going to get a real job?"

I was crushed. I had pretty much done what I wanted, traveling all over the country, and had done much for my age—but my personal accomplishments meant nothing to him.

And now, here I was, making the decision of where my father would be buried. I thought for a while and decided that if there was an open space near my brother, he would be placed there. If not, I would grant my aunt's wish. I called the cemetery where my brother was laid to rest and asked if there was a plot nearby.

They said, "Please hold for a moment." And then, after a long wait, "Yes, there is a plot one space over."

My sister-in-law, Connie, had made the decision two years earlier of where to put my brother Richard. It is a beautiful cemetery, located up along a mountain-type hill overlooking the valley. My brother loved the mountains. I, on the other hand, love the ocean.

There was one thing that I had to do as a son, and that was to make sure my sister Donna was there for the funeral even though she was very young when our parents divorced. I went over to my mom's house where she was visiting and told her that out of respect she should go. Even though she may not have been raised by him, he was her natural father that had brought her into this world. She agreed. Here was one more thing I did for my natural father, seeing to it that his only daughter, whom he loved, was there.

A month after my father's funeral, some of my friends came over to the Burbank house and said, "Ronnie, you've got to get out of the house! Come on! Let's go to the park; we'll carry you out of here if you don't get up out of that chair." I had been stuck in a zone for a few weeks after the funeral, and getting out and getting some fresh air and activity was a great idea.

I got up, and we all piled into the car and headed for the local park. I met a girl at the park while I was playing catch football with my friends. She was sitting alone under a tree, smoking a cigarette, and I walked up to her and asked for one after introducing myself.

She said, "Hello, glad to meet you, Ronnie. I'm Kay." She would be my girlfriend for the next two years. Leah would not come into my life for another two years from meeting Kay in the park under that tree. I was in motion again, thanks to the buddies that came over and suggested we go to the park and play some catch football.

It was time for a change, and soon the infamous Burbank house would no longer be in our lives and Danny would move back to Hollywood. He called me sometimes after he had just written a song, and over the phone (him being in Hollywood and me somewhere else in the area, which I stayed close to this time around because Kay lived in a town near the Burbank house called Simi Valley). He would play the new song and ask me, "What do you think?"

I would tell him exactly what I thought, which was not always what he wanted to hear. But most of the time I'd say, "It's a hit, top 5," or "Top 10," or "Number one with a Bullitt."

There was one special moment, way before acoustic-type renditions of songs were done after a song had landed on the charts as an artist or group's fully recorded hit with drums, piano, and electric bass guitar. For example, think of the super group The Eagles, when they did an MTV show called "Unplugged" (1994). Remember that? Well, I had driven out to Hollywood one day where Danny lived on—I think it was—Martel street.

I went in and we made some coffee, and he said, "Hey, Ronnie, check this out."

The single Danny wrote, called "Winners and Losers," was already out on the charts, and radio stations throughout America and across the Atlantic were playing it. I sat down and sipped my coffee while Dan played for me the "unplugged" version of the recorded song on his Ovation acoustic guitar.

He said, "This is how it sounded when I first wrote it." It was a slower version, and it was a great moment for me when he took the time to share it with me.

The Doberman Gang

There were a few times in my life that I came across the infamous dog the Doberman Pinscher. One time in my early 20s, I was dating a girl and went to pick her up at her house. I walked nonchalantly up the walkway, and when I knocked on the door, to my astonishment, two Doberman Pinschers pulled back the curtain of the large living room picture window with their snouts, one the left curtain and the other the right curtain. As I looked at the two Dobermans with their growling teeth, scratching and barking up a storm, I was thankful that there was a piece of glass protecting me from a fate worse than a grizzly bear! My date came out, and I remember her yelling at Sheba (one of the dogs) to settle down.

I said to her, "I guess you don't date much, do you."

There was another time, at a barbecue at the Burbank house, where there were two dogs sitting side by side near a bunch of guests hanging out on the backyard patio; just another pleasant evening in Southern California. I was sitting at the patio table, talking to a master of the martial arts—I think he was a seventh-degree black belt in Karate or Kung Fu, one of those types—and he, being the teacher he was, was just finishing up another lesson, using the analogy of a bug that had been crawling on the patio table towards me. I had just shooed it away with my hand, and he commented, "See, Ronnie, what you just did?"

I said, "What?"

He said, "You just fluffed that bug away even though it was in your turf and not a threat. You didn't squash it." Then the master of the arts said to me, "Ronnie, see the two dogs over there?"

I said, "Sure thing, I see them."

The two dogs were just getting their food, each one in its own dog bowl. One of the dogs was a short-haired Dachshund, the other a Doberman Pinscher.

The martial arts teacher said, "Now watch the little dog and you will see he is still eating. The larger dog is now finished with his food."

As he said the word "finished," I noticed the Doberman took a glance at the smaller dog's food bowl and then moved his snout toward the Weiner dog's bowl. The Dachshund growled, and the Doberman stepped back.

The martial arts master said to me, "The Doberman can eat that little dog as a snack, but the Dachshund stood his ground so the Doberman backed off."

I realized, as young as I was back then, that if anything became a threat then I was to stand my ground no matter how big the contender was. As far as the bug that I fluffed away, it was no threat; therefore, there was no need to display aggression, so I just moved it along its way.

There is an interesting motion picture that came out in 1973 called *The Doberman Gang*. It is definitely one of the most entertaining movies I have ever seen, and I remember it to this day.

A roadie's heart

My First Love

I met Leah around 1982, just as Jan Nash the psychic had predicted five years earlier. Leah was down from Sacramento where her parents lived and where she was raised, though the family was a transplant from Iowa. Simi Valley was where her sister lived and worked, and that's how I met Leah, through her sister.

Her sister Debbie, a waitress, was waiting on my table. I was by myself and single again. Kay, the girl I met under a tree in the park, had gone her own way. Just as my football buddies helped me get back in motion, Kay, a Sagittarius like me, dated me for about two years, which also kept me moving forward.

As I was eating, I chatted with Debbie. I of course mentioned that I was roadie for Hamilton, Joe Frank & Reynolds.

"Oh," she responded, "my husband plays guitar. Why don't you come over and meet him?" Her husband would turn out to be Mike Goldman, my Jewish buddy, a true definition of a friend!

I went over to Debbie's house to meet her husband Mike. I introduced myself to him and right away I could see that he was somebody that was a straight-up kind of guy, as I was now mingling with the public and no longer on the road constantly touring. Then, while I was hanging out with Mike in his living room, I saw in the distance a redheaded young woman. I thought that she was just fine as wine, and the fact that she was not a groupie, that I was meeting a young woman in a domestic situation, was very appealing to me. The longer I stayed off the road touring, the more I was enjoying being in the company of a woman, the same woman, for more than just one night.

Leah and I dated for a while, and then I introduced her to Danny Hamilton and his future wife Fredricka, as they both were now living together in the Hollywood area.

Danny often did gigs around town, and Leah and I would go catch him playing. One of the clubs we went to was D.B. Coopers, named after the famous man who parachuted out of a plane at just under 10,000 feet with $200,000 he demanded from the airline in exchange for the passengers he was holding hostage. They say he was never found. Anyway, this was a cool club, a really nice, comfortable, pub-type place.

After Leah and I arrived at the pub, we met Danny's brother Judd Hamilton and Judd's famous wife, Miss Caroline Munroe from London. Caroline was a very famous actress who did a lot of sci-fi movies like *The Golden Voyage of Sinbad* (1973). You can see her in one of the James Bond movies, *The Spy who Loved Me* (1977). She is strikingly beautiful.

I didn't know anything about Caroline when I was introduced to her; it was only later on that I noticed her on those late night movies and then recognized her in that James Bond movie. Hanging out with Caroline made me wonder how it would be to meet the actress Raquel Welch. Movie stars have not only a glow about them but also an energy that I imagine would be almost palpable for a loyal fan who tried to carry on a conversation with them. Caroline was just lovely.

So there we all were at the pub, sitting at a table, when Judd, a guitar player and singer just like his famous brother Danny, got up to play. I got up and sat in on drums. So there was Danny, Judd, myself and a bass player jamming away to Neil Diamond's song "Sweet Caroline" as Judd sang to his wife sitting in the audience. To this day, when I hear that song by Neil Diamond, I think on those great memories of jamming at D.B Coopers. I remember another time when all of us—Leah, Danny, Fredricka, and I—were sitting in a restaurant and I was trying to think of a radio name. Then Fredricka came up with Ronnie Rush!

I remember when Leah and I were out one night in a club in Simi Valley in Southern California, where we'd first met and went on our first date to drink, eat, and dance. She nudged me with her elbow and said, "You could do a better job than that guy up there in the DJ booth."

Since her sister was a waitress at the club, I told her sister to tell the manager that if he needed a part-time DJ to let me know. My career as a DJ began!

Years earlier, the "thing to do" for a band or group wanting to get discovered was to perform in clubs. So I took that concept and hoped that some program director from a radio station would walk into one of the nightclubs where I worked, approach me, and say, "Hey, you have a great voice. Would you like to work on the radio?"

But I was far from what the standards were for a radio DJ, something I would experience in the years ahead.

The Banditos

Through all of my life experiences, even walking in a lightning storm in the rain with only crackling thunder for company, I always had a sense that God was very well aware of me in the midst of it all and that if anything were to happen to me he would use his power to intervene. When we are asleep, we are at our most vulnerable. But I believe that God's hand is mighty and, most of all, above all evil that roams this earth day or night. We are protected, whether we are awake or in a deep sleep.

The time two banditos broke the door in at 3 am at a Motel 6 where Leah and I were staying was a life-changing experience. I'd had a job spinning records in the town of Monrovia, at the Howard Johnson high-rise hotel and restaurant. It was a pretty cushy job spinning records at the Howard Johnson Hotel and then heading up to the room where we stayed, all expenses paid, including a meal a day. When Hotel Howard Johnson (Ho Jo's, as we called it) said they were cutting the DJ booth and bringing in live entertainment, I had to break the news to Leah that we were going to have to pack up and move on.

The closest Motel 6 was in a nearby town called Azusa. Though I had walked the streets of Los Angeles where the famous Watts Tower was, I would not want to ever step foot in Azusa again. Watts is notorious for trouble in the heart of Los Angeles, also famous for the Watts riots of 1965 when the whole city of Los Angeles was burning.

We'd checked into a Motel 6, taking a few things in but leaving everything else that I owned in the car, including the hamper. Why the hamper? Maybe because it held more stuff, as the car I owned was that same hatchback Gremlin that was stolen (and recovered) that kept going and going like a tank. You know, one of those ugly cars that gets you where you need to go.

Looking back years later, it is apparent to me that having everything you own in your car while traveling is probably a red flag to any criminals on the lookout for travelers that might have available cash. Quite the contrary, however, we were poor.

We went to a nearby coffee shop for something to eat, and while we were waiting for our food to arrive, this black dude with no arms walked up to our table and asked me if I would help him to the bathroom. It was so long ago, I don't remember if I hesitated or looked at Leah with surprise, thinking, *This guy needs my help to piss?*

I went with him to the bathroom and helped him with his pants but told him there was no way I was going to hold it for him. He managed without me, and then I helped him pull his pants back up and went back to my table. That was just about the weirdest thing that's ever happened to me.

Leah and I finished our food and went back to the Motel 6. I guess we were thinking to stay about a day or two until we'd decided what we were going to do. With two beds, I decided Leah could stretch out on one and I on the other, and I took the bed closest to the door.

We had settled into sleep, but at 3 am, sleeping butt-naked, I was rudely awakened from a deep sleep when two men kicked in the door. I felt an internal force pull my body up out of bed as I rose up, and then I was instantly at the door, holding them off from entering the room.

Still coming out of a deep sleep, I only vaguely heard one of the banditos telling me that he wanted to use the telephone. All the while, I was pushing the door shut against the two banditos, who were pushing and shoving their way in and causing the door to open about 3 or 4 inches before I would slam it shut again. This went on a few times before I realized that the lock in the doorjamb had been totally ripped out. My attempts at closing the door and trying to get it to catch the locking device were not going to work.

I put all my weight against the door to hold them off, keeping the door closed as if pure evil or the devil himself was on the other side. The two banditos were still trying to get in, and I knew they were not going to give up. I turned toward the second bed and saw Leah sitting up, watching what was taking place.

I said, "Leah, my gun! It's under the bed!"

At that moment, the pressure on the other side of the door disappeared completely. I waited a few seconds and then opened the door all the way. The banditos were gone.

"Gather your stuff," I told Leah. "We're leaving."

It was now about 3:30 am. We got in the car and headed to a payphone. I got lucky and found a functioning pay phone (it always seemed that when I needed to make a call from a pay phone in an average day-to-day situation the cord was cut or the phone speaker was unscrewed or some prankster had put some smelly substance on the earpiece, if you know what I mean). I called Danny Hamilton, and he picked up. I told him what had happened.

He said, "Come on over. You and Leah can stay the night."

This was around the time when MTV had just started launching their music videos. We went over to Danny and Fredricka's house, and Leah and I lay down together. Just before we fell asleep, I could feel the two of us trembling, but I knew without a doubt that we were now safe.

My First Taste of Sacramento (1983)

I drove up to Sacramento the very first time with Leah, just to visit, drop her off at her parents, and continue to a club gig at Stewart Anderson's Steakhouse further up in another town. The gig did not pan out, so I stalled out and had to stay with Leah and her parents because there was nowhere for me to go. When I left Los Angeles, it was, for the moment in time, for good. I was moving forward then, and my habit was, to use an expression to make my point, to go and not look back.

There was one thing I noticed about Sacramento immediately: all the trees! Trees were everywhere. I looked in the Sacramento Bee, the local paper, and the other newspaper, at that time called The Union, but there was no work. I felt like a fish out of water and it wasn't even Friday. (Catholic joke.) I think it was because of the way I had arrived, like a loser, for lack of a better word, even imposing a little.

But Leah was a trouper. She made me feel as comfortable as possible, and we did things together, going to the movies and out to dinner on occasion. We went out as a family, Leah, her dad, mom, and I, to a movie and saw an incredible showing called *The Man from Snowy River*.

Time passed for a month or two when the reality set in that I was in a strange town not knowing anyone but Leah and without a job, and Leah suggested I return to Los Angeles, a more familiar territory geographically, to regroup and see what came of it. So, with everything I owned in my car, I eventually went back to Los Angeles alone to live.

I did, however, practice my radio DJ skills while I was visiting with Leah and her parents. It was not all a waste of time. I made phone calls to some of the Sacramento radio stations. A program director (PD) at a station I would eventually work for, years later when I returned to Sacramento for good, told me, "Ronnie, you have to work the outlining areas before you can enter the

Sacramento market. Get some experience for a few years and check back then."

This key information the PD gave me, as casual as it seemed at the time, would be worth gold to me later. Just as a lighthouse guides ships around the globe, his statement would guide me along the path I had set for myself in my future career of radio.

The Arrival

Los Angeles is a high-energy town, and if you were going to survive the City of Angels, you had to be working some kind of job—any job that would bring in money in order to eat. Being young and living in a big city, it was a constant hustle for me to get through each day.

I had the opportunity to move north from L.A. to where Leah was still staying with her parents in a town where I knew no one but her. But she was the love of my life. I had been in love before and had been "Fallin' in Love" on tour, but this was special because I could be with this person every day. Not only that, but I wanted to be with her and she with me. To me, there is nothing so incredible as to have a love for someone and to have that love returned. I have—and I'm sure you have too—experienced that "one-way street" kind of love where you like someone and they don't feel the same or they like you and you don't reciprocate. The two-way street on the other hand is bliss.

I finally was able to make arrangements with one of the local night club and hotel chains, Howard Johnson, that had an in-house DJ booth in Sacramento, and I was able to make sure I had a job before leaving Southern California, which had been home since I was 5 years old. This was a life-changing turn for me. I had no idea of what lay ahead other than the love I had for my girl, a job, my car, $50.00 in my pocket, and the place Leah had found for me to live. An older woman, who was a nurse, owned a home in Sacramento and rented out rooms, and I was one of her new tenants.

I arrived in Sacramento, California on March 4, in the year of our Lord 1984. The #1 song that week was "Footloose" by Kenny Loggins.

Despite my optimism and forward-focused mindset, I did struggle for a couple years before I found my groove, but as I look back on the 27 years that have passed since my arrival, I can see a lot of things I had a hand in creating regarding the people I met along the way and their successes. Had I managed to continue down Highway 99 South back to Los Angeles the times I tried to leave, their lives would not be the same. It's kind of like that story you have probably seen on TV, *It's a Wonderful Life* with Jimmy Stewart. Had he not existed, others' lives would not be the same. Whether we are aware or not, we do touch the lives of others in one way or another, large or small, noticed or unnoticed. Imagine introducing someone to a friend of yours, and they get married and have a child, and you meet that child for the first time knowing while you're hugging the kid that if it were not for you, the child you're hugging would not be there to hug.

To this day, my survival has hinged on factors like introducing people to each other, which has led to what we'll call my inner circle of friends, which kept me from moving back to Los Angeles even though I got the urge several times to pack up everything and head back. We are all born with a family and siblings that we have no say or control over, but when we get older we have control over who our "inner circle" of friends will be. I managed to fight the strong urge to return home to southern California because of them.

It was good that I didn't pack up everything and move back to Los Angeles, even though many of my pleasant memories are there. I managed to gain ground in Sacramento by staying and building friendships and getting involved in things that would keep me busy and carry me through those times when I did get the urge to pack up and go. I did visit my old home, though, and over time I found that a few days in Los Angeles was enough and I could not wait to return back to my adopted hometown of Sacramento.

Back then, they called Sacramento "Cow Town." That slang remains today, as do the cliques. Sacramento is a clique town, and I was a Los Angeles transplant. If you don't know anyone, it can be quite a challenge to settle in, especially since there was a gypsy in me that was tempted to want to travel to go find a concert tour. But I kept at it. Sometimes, when I would get to a leveling off period where I felt I was not making progress or reaching even a moderate sign of success, I would psyche myself out to think I had just arrived in town, and that would give me a boost as I looked around and saw where I was in life and what I had accomplished and compared that with what I'd had when I arrived in Sacramento: a job and 50 dollars in my pocket. It helped break the cycle of boredom, at least.

Doing this self-motivation technique that I developed helped me clip my recent baggage that was accumulating as a negative like a long train of hundreds of cars seems endless while you are waiting for the caboose. In other words, I found a way to drag all of that around while still having in my mind all of the current experiences, getting rid of the weight of the long tail but keeping what I learned in mind, making me feel like I'd lightened the load. I'm not getting too heavy am I? And no, I was not a hobo on that train in my mind. The gypsy still remains!

As I was trying to settle in Sacramento and more time had passed, I just did not want to look back and be discouraged by the flat track record. Having the feeling of a fresh start, of just arriving but having all my current experience, seemed to work for me in getting "over the hump" to settle in. I was laying down a foundation.

I don't know what it was that made me feel weighed down sometimes, but as the years started to accumulate I was getting to feel like I was in a rut. Maybe that's why people go on vacation, to get away for a while and then return back to their familiar daily routines. For me, it was just the opposite; I was always on the move. I had to give myself a chance to try to settle in and make a go at the stationary life. My desire was to stay.

I had been on the move my entire life until I met Leah in Los Angeles. Her mom and dad lived in Sacramento, where she was raised, though Leah was born in Iowa. I was 29 when I met her, and she was in her late teens, having just turned 19. My mom knew how much of a gypsy I was and about the many women I had had in my life, but she knew that Leah was special to me because I brought her to meet my mom. When a son brings home a girl to meet his mother, it's an unspoken word between mother and son that the girl is special. Now, whether a mother likes the girl her son brings home is another challenge, but Mom liked Leah.

I had traveled all over the USA, and I'd found that people in general are good. There are definitely some assholes to watch out for, but overall there are more good than bad. I remember that it was reported on the news that everyone was very courteous and nice the day after 9/11, the attack on the World Trade Center in New York, the great city John Lennon loved to call home.

Then, within a few weeks, it was back to the usual grind of driving, with people honking their horns, giving the middle finger, and hurrying to wherever it was they were headed.

Just today, as I was on Hwy 50, minding my own business in the right lane and going the speed limit for that lane, 55 mph, I saw in my rearview mirror that there were a couple of people in a car behind me that were waving their arms for me to hurry it up. They came around and, as they passed me, the passenger gave me the middle finger, a real popular sign here in America. I wonder if it means the same thing around the world. We all get caught up in the grind, forgetting our time is short here on planet Earth. Be kind.

Sometimes Love Comes with a Crown of Thorns

I have heard many times, and maybe you have as well, that it's better to have loved and lost than to never have loved at all. For some reason, this always makes me think about the black widow spider. I learned while growing up as a kid that when black widows mate, the female spider bites off the head of the male spider, killing him instantly. There is no way of knowing whether or not the male spider knows about this trait of the female, unless there is a third spider watching, but there are still today many spiders, as there are men and women on the earth. Life is full of experiences. If there were no ups then there would be no downs.

Just a few months after arriving in Sacramento, I went to pick Leah up for dinner at her parents' house, and when I got to the front door and knocked, she answered that she was not going to dinner and that she wanted me off her property.

I was devastated. I called later to see if she would talk, but she would have no part of it. Her father even got on the phone and said that he would get a restraining order on me if I called anymore. The family had kicked me to the curb. I had come all this way to make a life for myself and Leah and had put the gypsy in me in the bottle for safekeeping. It's a very lonely feeling when people you have come to know and trust and consider to be family turn on you, without regard for your welfare, for a reason unknown to you.

But that was it; it was over. Leah and I had just returned from Los Angeles a month earlier, where we'd gone for Mother's Day to visit my mom and sisters. I remember we all went to the local park and hung out for the Mother's Day gathering before Leah and I drove back to Sacramento. A few weeks later, it was over.

To this day 27 years later, (as of 2011) I still don't know exactly what happened. You think back—Was it this or that? Did I say something? You compare and guess and think to the point where it takes you into a tailspin and all your energy is drained on a daily basis because your mind cannot comprehend why the bond of trust was broken.

It was all I could do to get through the day. I visited friends in Los Angeles, and they could not believe she'd left. When I talked, it was always about Leah. There was no other subject. I would go on and on about what happened, analyzing over and over what could have broken the special bond that had melded us together in love.

I'm sure some of my very close friends, whom I'd known for many years, thought at the time that I was going through some kind of hell.

You know, I don't think we ever really, really know anyone else's pain except our own. When somebody you love turns their back on you and rejects you, it's about the darkest time in the world. I thought, had Leah died, I would have been able to handle it better, as I had much experience with the finality of death. But Leah was still alive and did not want to hear from me ever again.

One of the last things she said on the phone to me was that she had been dumped before by other guys. I just could not believe that this was the same person who had written me a beautiful card that read, *Dear Ron, thanks so much for being so understanding and caring for me the way you do, you deserve the very best out of life and I want to be with you always.*

That pretty much says everything. I had arrived in town with only $50 in my pocket and a job, and I knew no one but her. Today, I say I know everyone but her and have only two quarters to rub together. (Just kidding about the two quarters.) The only thing over the years that I have kept is a gold cross and chain she gave me and that I had a priest bless for me. As she handed it to me many years ago, she said, "This is my gift to you to protect you."

My reply was, "I will keep it forever and I want to be buried with it."

I tried to leave Sacramento twice in the years it took for me to get over the love we had had for each other. She had, like a Paul McCartney tune says, "pulled me out of time, hung me on a line," ("Maybe I'm Amazed", #10 in 1977). It was my loyalty that kept me wanting her and that morally would not allow me to leave her. I don't know if this was something that I was taught in Catholic school or not, but I could not even think that I would do something like leaving her out in the middle of a desert. I cherished the ground she walked on. She was someone I wanted to be with always. We fit like a puzzle. I was comfortable with her; she was my best friend. I thought we'd had an everlasting love.

I remember the great time we spent on Malibu beach together. She and I swam about a half a mile out to sea, and then she asked me, "Are you ready to go back to shore?"

I said, "Yes, let's get back and walk the beach."

As we were walking the beach, a man was jogging from the other direction and was headed straight for us. I saw that he was not going to go around us, so I moved out of the way just in time, and as he brushed by me, I saw it was actor Ryan O'Neal. Up ahead, we went underneath one of the beachfront houses and came out about 15 minutes later. As we were walking back to our car, it struck me that the two of us had been out about half a mile in the ocean, and I looked at her and realized she had helped me overcome my fear of the ocean. Still to this day, when I watch the Discovery Channel's *Shark Week*, I think about the two of us out there in the mighty ocean.

It's times like that and so many other moments that you reflect on when you are now standing alone. Just listen to Elvis Presley's song "Memories" (#35 in 1969). I don't want to sound religious or anything, but the words *faith*, *hope*, and *love*, with *love* being the most powerful of the three, came to my mind often.

I tried hard to leave Sacramento a couple of times within an eighteen month period after the breakup, but fate would bring me back each time. What a vivid reminder of that momentum when I saw Al Pacino (my favorite actor, by the way) say in *The Godfather 3*, motioning with his hands, "Just when I think I'm out, they pull me back in."

I tried to go to the California-Oregon border. I even went on a late-night drive down Highway 99 from Sacramento to Los Angeles with everything I owned in my car, but I only got as far as the town of Galt, about 30 minutes out of Sacramento, before this really weird feeling came over me that told me I was doing the wrong thing by leaving. It wasn't the feeling that I was leaving someone behind; rather, it seemed to be telling me that going back home to Los Angeles was not right. As I look back, I can see clearly those people in my close circle of friends who would not have prospered and those that would not have their children had I continued down Highway 99 or stayed on the California-Oregon border.

I would have swum through shark-infested waters for Leah. As time went on, I was able to not feel so bad and to not think I was abandoning her by moving on without her.

On one occasion, I was working the nightclub scene back in Simi Valley just outside Los Angeles (before I finally made the big move to Cow Town to start my life with her) and Leah and I were renting a room with some other people around our age. I must have drank some bad water; maybe it was delivered to the DJ booth by one of the waitresses when the bartender gave me water in a glass that had gotten some of the shelf moisture or bacteria into it, or maybe I drank a standing glass of water from the nightstand that had gotten tainted somehow. Whatever the source, within a day or so, I was throwing up, then trying to drag myself out of bed with all my strength, totally out of it with a high fever, dehydrated, and with diarrhea so bad I tried to make it to the toilet but missed by a few feet.

I was lying face down on the floor when Leah found me. She helped me get back into bed and stayed at my side the whole time I was sick. She even went back to the bathroom and cleaned up the poop. She remained at my side throughout my fever, and when the day came when I was able to travel, she took me to the doctor to give a bowel sample. They tested the sample I gave them in a Styrofoam cup, and when the results came back they told me I'd ingested some microbe parasite that, if left untreated, would have killed me.

Most of the time we think when we're ill that we'll get better over a period of a few days, but this is not always the case.

The doctor prescribed a medicine to kill the parasite they'd identified in the poop test. Thank God for modern science! Now I'm very careful about what I'm drinking and where it came from and how fresh it is, and if I don't know, it gets thrown away pronto!

I remember telling Leah on the phone, after she told me goodbye, that I would wait for her.

Leah replied, "You would be wasting your life."

A year after that very statement, my mom would pass away in June 1985.

When One Knows You So Well Even Over the Phone

Leah, the girl I fell in love with, the girl I'd introduced to my closest friends on the planet (Danny Hamilton and Fredricka), left me on June 1st, 1984, which happened to be Danny's birthday. I always made sure to wish Danny a happy birthday, as his birthday is the same as that of one of my favorite movie stars, Marilyn Monroe.

I called Danny to wish him a happy birthday that evening and he said to me, "You and Leah broke up, right?"

I said, "Yes, but how can you know? It just happened."

"Because I can hear it in your voice," Danny said.

I remember one night when Danny was recording in the studio with a first engineer at the controls and I was thinking about something, not really looking at Danny while he was putting down a vocal track.

Suddenly, Danny stopped in his tracks (no pun intended) and said, "Ronnie, if you're going to be thinking about something other than what we're doing then go outside." He added, "You're distracting me."

"But I'm not talking!" I said.

He said, "Your thoughts are distracting me."

So I got focused on the session. I thought later about how in tune he was with energy. I once asked him about a book that was on the coffee table in his living room, and he said it was the *Urantia Book*, about how the universe was created. I picked it up, read about one paragraph, and then had to set it down because I didn't understand the language even though it was written in English.

In the very early days of my tenure in radio, just after graduating broadcasting school, around 1986, I would call Danny and I would play my air check over the phone. The radio station had a recorder where you could slip in a blank cassette and, when you pop the mic, it would turn on and start recording. Then, when you finished talking, you could turn the mic off and the recorder would stop. So after an hour-long show, the tape would have recorded the intro to the songs and, if you talked at the end of a song, it would have recorded the ending as well as you talked out of the song.

"COOL 101, that was Hamilton, Joe Frank, & Reynolds for Sheila in Sacramento, who's sending her love to Brian, and Brian, she tells me to tell you, 'Boo Boo for you!' It's 6:25 in the city; boy, I hope she wasn't calling from a baseball game. It's yo boo boo Ronnie Rush on COOL 101!"

So after about a 4-hour show, while the tape machine was recording, anyone listening to the tape later would hear a 4-hour show in about 7 minutes. This 7-minute air check is what I would play back to Danny on my landline phone, and he would listen on his landline phone.

Danny said to me, "You picked those songs on your own and played them in the order you decided to play them in."

I said "Yes, but how did you know?"

Dan said, "Because I know you and the way the songs are in order as they played tell me that it's you."

Today, as I look back on that moment, I believe that the only way he could have known what I was actually doing at the radio station studio was by leaving his body and hanging out with me at the radio station studio, like an astral projection, because I was the only one that knew that the program director allowed me to play any song in any order as long as I did not repeat a song during my shift.

Point to Ponder

I heard one time early on, when I was in my 20s, from an older person of wisdom, "I am a little bit of everyone I met." It's amazing how we take from life without realizing it the very things we look at more closely once we have gotten older.

Fran La Blanc

Fran was the first person outside of my music world of DJing in Sacramento night clubs to give me a job. I worked for a while as a salesman with her advertising company. I had no family around , but I was now gaining ground and purpose that kept me from just packing up and going on the impulse that "nothing is going on," which would have made it time to move on, a concept that the gypsy in me seemed to reveal to me many times.

I remember Fran and her girlfriends would take the time to come to where I was spinning records at the nightclubs I worked at in and around Sac-town, and she would walk up to the DJ booth, request a song, and, with her hand over her heart, say, "Ronnie, your voice." This was a precious moment for me as I had not yet committed my life to a radio career yet. Some years later, Fran passed away from liver failure, but her sincere comment has never been forgotten.

Ross F. duClair

I had been working in outside sales for Fran, which gave me an opportunity to meet the cliquish folks of Sacramento, when another one of fate's ways of getting me to the next level kicked into play in my life. This was just after Leah had left me, and while I was still bummed, I was determined to make Fran glad that she'd hired me. I walked into a Mom & Pop video store when the counter person and the owner happened to both be standing at the service counter, and I gave my sales pitch to both of them at the same time.

The owner, Ross, immediately said, "Where do I sign? We were just waiting for the very next person to enter our store for some advertising."

Eventually, in December 1984, I became Ross' General Manager. That job ended just a few months later, but Ross wrote an eloquent letter of recommendation for me. The letter told my future employer that I had so much enthusiasm and talent in promotions that since my hire, the store I managed, which had lagged behind since its opening, had now surpassed the main store. Store #2 was sold, however, so there was no need for me to operate it as the owner would be coming back to run the original store.

Finally, having made my mark in Sacramento, I was on my way down the long road that would bring me to where I am today. I remember my step-father saying to me, "Ronnie, if you can count your friends on one hand, you're doing pretty good, son."

I would say to my step-father today that Ross surely had a hand in getting me kick-started in what I would eventually be calling Sacramento, my adopted hometown, which kept the gypsy in me grounded for a little while longer. When Leah said goodbye, there was no one in Sacramento that was family; they were all in Los Angeles. But Fran La Blanc was like an aunt to me, and Ross became like another big brother, and their love and support kept me in Sacramento. It was another small miracle that those two came into my life.

Little did I know that fate later would have Ross at the very radio station where I worked 13 years later, even though radio was not on my radar when he and I met. Ross had become the assistant chief engineer at Chancellor Broadcasting and eventually became Chief Engineer of what is now called Clear Channel Radio. I was rockin' the air waves on Sacramento's Oldies station, Cool 101.1, and as I came out of the studio for a break, there was Ross!

I said, "Hey, wow, what are you doing here? I haven't seen you since 1985!"

Ross said, "Well, Ronnie, I'm the assistant chief engineer here, and you sound really great!"

Keep on Keepin' on

Border of California and Oregon

I had answered an ad in the Sacramento Bee newspaper for a radio DJ gig just on the California/Oregon border. Even though all expenses would be paid while I was there working the station, I only stayed in that town for a few hours. I arrived at the station, went on the air and played some country songs, and then went back to the hotel to eat. While I was eating and pondering the goodness of all-expenses-paid food and lodging, I couldn't shake the feeling that country music was not for me.

After my meal, I went up to my room and lay down to meditate on the whole idea of moving from where I was, Sacramento, to a very strange and hillbilly-type town with logger trucks coming and going. I had everything to my name still packed in my car.

As I was lying on the bed, I looked around the room and remembered something my mom had said while we were growing up when she was in the kitchen cooking, spatula moving in her hand to emphasize what she was saying and gesturing as most Italians do when they are talking. She told us that the losers of the world wind up in a room with a swinging light bulb, and mom timed the pointing of the spatula in my direction as she spoke, totally making it clear that she did not want that for me. Another one of my mom's famous descriptions was of a person with "not a pot to piss in or a window to throw it out of."

While thinking on all these things, the hair on the back of my neck stood straight out like the hair on the backs of two alley cats about to get into a brawl. I had no conscious control over this. I'd heard the phrase, "It would make the hair on the back of your neck stand straight out," and it made me feel like I was in some kind of danger.

This experience with the hair on the back of the neck came with its own built-in warning. I remember a similar experience associated not with danger, exactly, but with the feeling that I should not proceed any further. I was waxing cars in Los Angeles and had to return a hearse back to the mortuary. I was a little concerned that I would get there after dark. I didn't mind the smell of the flowers that lingered in the vehicle, even though it had just been washed and waxed on the outside and cleaned and vacuumed on the inside, but the folks that work in a mortuary are cut from a different piece of cloth. That type of work is not for me. I just wanted to get in and get out and be done while it was still light. This was just a few years before keyboardist Alan Dennison would give us a tour of his family mortuary business, but dealing with the dead wasn't appealing to me even after that.

I was arriving just in time to park and go up to the office of the funeral home before it closed, and I figured I'd be able to get out quickly while there was some daylight left. I opened the front door of the mortuary office and walked in and down the hall, calling for the owner.

As I reached a set of stairs at the end of the hall, I saw a dim light at the top of the staircase. So I went slowly up the stairs, all the way to the top, and saw a man at a desk writing with the desk lamp on low.

I said "I'm here to drop off the hearse. Here are the keys, and if you have the check I'll be on my way."

The funeral director stopped and looked up at me with a sincere smile and said, "Yes, I'll write you a check. It will only be a minute."

I was thinking all that time about how quickly I would have to get out to make it back before it was too dark. A few long minutes later, however, the check was written.

As the director handed it to me, he said, "Can you find your way out all right?"

With a brave smile, I said, "Oh, sure. No problem."

I thanked him and walked back down the stairs, down the hall, made a right turn and went down that hall, and then came to a door and opened it.

It was not the exit.

It was a dark room, and I only got one foot in before I got that gut-feeling that I was not allowed to be in that room. Could it have been a waiting room for the dead? I don't know and didn't want to find out. All I knew was that I needed to get gone! I retraced my steps and found the exit, and yes, it was pitch black outside.

Anyway, at the Oregon border hotel, not long after I got that feeling of the hair standing on the back of my neck, I packed up the small carry case I had brought up with me and my feet were doing double time as I went down the steps to the hotel lobby, right up to the front desk.

I said, "Thank you for everything, but I'm going to play the hits. Country music is not for me."

And with that, I left the area and returned to Sacramento with everything I owned in my car. I regrouped back in Cow Town, and Sacramento became my adopted hometown. That was before I had graduated from broadcasting school and was still working the clubs as a DJ; these were my early days struggling to settle into Sacramento.

I think that if I hadn't listened to the inner voice, my inner warning system, I may not have made it a week there on the Oregon border. I could have been robbed and beaten to death had I been influenced to stay because of the unique situation of all expenses paid, free food, hotel, and job! But I was not going to have any part of it due to the warning of the hair on the back of my neck. Now, had I not felt that strong sense of danger, I may have just tried the "country thing" for a while, knowing that going back to Sacramento with hardly any money, no job, and no place to go would be a challenge.

It has been so long ago since I returned to Sacramento that I don't remember how or when I arrived or whether I found a place to crash on a friend's couch. I think the experience of those challenging days kept me in one place for a long time, though I still get the urge to get back on the road touring.

All of us, you and me, have struggled in our lives to get to the next level, whatever the goals we have set for ourselves. Even after we have been told to have the big balance in the savings account and money in the checking with 6 months of backup funds in case of an emergency, we all have those ghosts that come back to haunt us, and the memories come to us as strongly as they did back when we were struggling or just squeaking by. Why we keep such a memory—or should I say, it keeps us—I don't know.

I'm sure you have those little private indicators that alert you when you have come out of your struggle or a tough time. I have several indicators. If I see toilet paper in the cupboard, for example, I know things are pretty good. I say this because during the hardship of trying to settle in Sacramento, there were times I had to borrow a roll of toilet paper from my roommate until I got my next paycheck. Maybe for you it's toothpaste or a certain kind of food that wasn't in the refrigerator. Think about it, because all my rich friends have their own little indicators that have stayed with them.

My friend Sammy, for example, said he and his family went without electricity in his motor home and no one came to help. So maybe for Sam, the power bill being paid is an indicator of moderate success (regardless of whether or not there are thousands in his bank account).

Aside from all the hardships that followed, my breakup with Leah notwithstanding, settling into a new town takes you in its own way on a hard road to haul.

My Jewish buddy Mike Goldman, now living in Sacramento, who was married to Leah's sister, Debbie, got divorced a while after Leah and I broke up. Together they had two kids, a boy and a girl. Debbie also had a son from a previous marriage, but my buddy Mike Goldman treated all the children with a father's love, as I observed on many occasions when they were a family and I was invited over for dinner. When Mike Goldman and Debbie separated, Mike let me stay with him, which kept me off the streets and from having to sleep in my car. Like I said, it's not easy settling into a new town.

I soon got on my feet and, with a job, got my own apartment. A while after, Mike Goldman called me and said, "Ronnie, my son and I have no place to go."

I said, "Mike, come stay with me. I have a two-bedroom apartment, and you and your son can have the other bedroom."

Life is a circle. This was just after my mom passed away, and Mike, being the good buddy he was, had called Leah on my kitchen phone at my request to tell her that my mom was gone. He hung up the phone and said, "Ronnie, she knows."

The fact that she didn't volunteer to speak to me was something I expected, but it would have been nice to hear her voice and talk to her as a friend would. But it was not meant to be. There are no words for the awful feeling I experienced when Leah did not step up for me after Mike hung up the phone. It's worse than the alone feeling that all of us have experienced once or twice in our lives. It's worse than the cringe feeling. I don't really know the word for it, but I do know how it feels, and I surely don't ever want to experience that feeling again. (Of course, the male black widow spider never gets a second chance, so things aren't too bad.)

All I know is that the feeling is terrible, horrible, and I have some idea of why a person would jump the Bay Bridge after a breakup or find some other means of getting rid of the overwhelming feeling that pounds at you and goes through your body and paralyzes you with total rejection.

Mike's call to Leah was in July 1985. It took almost 13 months after Leah and I broke up for fate to bring Mike and his son to my apartment, but thanks to Mike Goldman, word got to Leah that my mom had passed away.

About that time in 1985, Live Aid was broadcast worldwide. Don Johnson of TV show *Miami Vice* fame was hot as a pancake, and when he came out on stage the fans that were in the audience gave out a roar! He was one of the many Hollywood stars and famous musicians of the decade that would certify and legitimize the concert, which simultaneously was at another concert stage in London with a huge crowd bringing London's famous to the stage to perform for world hunger.

Live Aid was a dual-venue concert that was held on July 13, 1985. The event was organized by Bob Geldof and Midge Ure to raise funds for relief in the ongoing Ethiopian famine. Billed as the "global jukebox," the event was held simultaneously in Wembley Stadium, London, where it was attended by 72,000 people, and in the John F. Kennedy Stadium in Philadelphia, PA, which was attended by about 99,000 people. On the same day, concerts inspired by the initiative took place in other countries such as Australia and Germany. It was one of the largest-scale satellite link-ups and television broadcasts of all time: an estimated 2 billion viewers across 60 countries watched the live broadcast.

I'm thinking right now about how people say, when they bump into people they haven't seen in years, "Wow, it's a small world." But when you have to feed those who are starving around the world, then it's a big world! Looking back on that moment as a concert promoter now myself, I find that those organizers, Bob Geldof and company, were kings of promotion. I believe Bill Graham, the famous concert promoter for northern California, was there in support of the day's production as well.

Point to Ponder

I have to say that all the years of being raised in Los Angeles and Hollywood with all the friends I had cultivated made it hard for me once I'd settled in Sacramento because there were times the memories were so strong, almost like a yearning for a drug, that I wanted to sell everything but the clothes on my back and move back home to Southern California. I had worked out a strategy, though, which was to just go and visit for a day or so and then return back to Sacramento. The greatest part of those trips was the drive, because they gave me time to think as I enjoyed the scenery and stops along the way. The strong urge to sell everything and return to Los Angeles, where all my cherished memories were, faded over time, but the gypsy still remained inside me.

A Psychic Connection

I knew, as did my sisters and (I'm sure) my mother, that her time was short. I was sitting at the kitchen table one day on a visit, and I looked right at my mom, knowing her condition, and said, "Mom, please don't misunderstand what I'm getting ready to say, but I am your son, so I know you will understand my question."

I said to her, "Mom, if there is any way to communicate with me after you pass, will you try to communicate with me?"

She paused for a moment, then looked me right in the eye and said, "Sure, son, I will."

That was the end of that topic. I never got any closer with her to the subject of death, never had a one-on-one discussion about it.

One of the topics my mom and I had discussed was how she would get out of a ticket. So that was the most recent theme of conversation my mom and I had in person when I last visited her just before I got the call.

When I got "the call" in June of 1985, I was in Sacramento, and it was around 8 pm. I was at my favorite coffee shop where a bunch of us would hang out. Thomas, the manager, went over to the ringing phone answered it, then motioned for me to pick up the phone. It was my sister's husband telling me that my mom had slipped into a coma and that I needed to get to Los Angeles ASAP!

Nothing was open to get a rental car. Airports were closed, as this was 13 years before Sacramento would become an international airport. With no other options, I jumped into my sports car and hauled ass down Highway 99 to Los Angeles. I stopped once for gas along the way, in Fresno, and then I was back on the road again nonstop to the hospital.

I remember thinking that when I got there, I would talk her out of the coma with my voice. Surely she would recognize my voice and awaken. I was making good time from when I left Sacramento, doing about 75 miles an hour, maybe 80. And just as I thought to myself, *Damn, I'm making great time,* all of a sudden, to my left was a highway patrolman cruising at the same speed as me.

I thought then, *Shit, I can't stop. I got to get to the hospital and talk my mother out of her coma.* At that moment, while I was looking at the patrolman who was sitting in the passenger seat, he looked right at me, staring me down, and with his right palm facing down, moved his hand downward, giving me a sign to slow it down! I immediately obeyed and brought my speed down, and they continued on ahead of me. As their taillights faded in the distance, I looked to see what time it was and the digital clock said 10:30 pm.

I finally arrived at the hospital in Los Angeles, totally stressed out from the six-hour drive from Sacramento. There was no one around. My adrenalin must have been racing at 3000 rpm. Looking around, I wondered, *Could this hospital be closed?* I went into an area where I thought a doctor or nurse would be, looking for some sign of someone. Finally, a nurse came around the nurse's station, and I told her who I was and that I wanted to see my mom so I could talk her out of her coma! I knew she would recognize my voice. The nurse asked that I sit down, saying that the doctor would be right out.

I said, "I've been sitting for the last six hours. I'll just wait standing."

Then the doctor came out and said, "Maybe you should sit down."

I told the doctor what I had just told the nurse, that I'd been sitting for the past 6 hours and I wanted to talk my mom out of her coma.

The doctor said to me "Ronnie, your mom has passed away."

Those words, so final. There would be no bringing my mother out of her coma. The angels had taken her from the earth.

I asked "What time did she pass away?"

"At 10:30 pm," he told me. I realized that that moment had been when the highway patrol car was riding alongside of me.

Mom outlived the doctor's prediction by a year and a half. I have now outlived both my parents; Mom was a young 50 when she passed away, when I was about 31, and my Sicilian father was also 50 when he died, though I was

26. I'm now 57. It's Mother's Day as I write this, and there's an old saying that goes like this: "The hand that rocks the cradle rules the world!"

The Lost Years

Between the ages of 23 and 31, I lost seven people in my immediate family. It doesn't get any easier each time you hear the dreaded news that there has been a death in the family. The road that life takes you down is not always paved in gold, but it is a road that must be traveled. There is no turning back; this road is a one-way street and you can only continue forward, as dark as it may seem.

Dark clouds came upon me at each of the deaths of those years, and even having experience dealing with them doesn't make it easy to shake off the mourning. The experience just enabled me to know about how long the clouds would last. I had figured out that it took four seasons just for the dark clouds to be gone, but the sorrow always remained, only fading with time but never forgotten. Those first four seasons are crucial, and being unprepared for the journey can lead a person on a permanently dark road, such as to drugs and alcohol or even their own death. There are processes and stages of grieving that you must go through; otherwise, you are just delaying what you will eventually have to deal with later on.

Losing someone that is very close to you, especially if it is sudden, clips your being. If you decide not to participate in the wake, attend the funeral, or even take that walk to the cemetery, there are consequences later on. I won't go into it as this is a book about a roadie and those experiences on the road and what happens, but having experienced this delayed effect myself, I just say go!

If you deny your fear and embrace that the person you loved is dead, even though it may be painful in thought or even physically stressful, you will be purged through the process and you can carry the memory of their passing in your mind. Don't be in denial; admit that they have physically gone from the earth. Rejecting this is not good emotionally; it becomes like a negative energy within you that, over time, is a burden on the mind, body, and soul.

Try to find an outlet that allows you to face the loved one's passing, be it the wake, the funeral, or even a private visit to the cemetery. You will persevere and come out of it okay. Each time I got word of another death, I remember thinking, *Jesus, not again!* But you have no choice in the matter. You just deal with it as best you can regardless of the past. I worry about those who are alone and have no strong religious background to fall back on.

When it came to my mother's passing, I knew that it would be sooner rather than later because we had warning. About a year after I arrived in Sacramento, and my mother passed away from breast cancer at the age of 50 I had been through several deaths in my family already, and a metamorphosis was taking place within me, one that led to strength.

My first true love, Leah, along with my sisters and their boyfriends, were all sitting in the waiting area of the hospital. In those days, you could smoke in and around the waiting area. So when the doctor came out of the operating room, removing his mask as he approached us, some of us were smoking a cigarette.

The doctor said, shaking his head, with all of us looking up at him and hanging on his every word, "Your mother has six months to live, and if you kids can stop smoking, do it as soon as possible."

Leah put out her cigarette immediately, and I think that was her last puff. I don't know if it was because she was a left-hander, but she stopped and put her cigarette out as soon as the doctor made his pitch about quitting. We right-handers continued to smoke. I eventually quit (cold turkey) 15 years later, on February 1, 1999.

As the doctor spoke about the prognosis of mom having "smoker's cancer," I couldn't help saying to the doctor that my mom had quit smoking some 15 years earlier; she told me so herself. The doctor replied, "Its secondhand smoke."

When I moved up to Sacramento, I called and visited my mom every chance I got, as I knew her time was short. I remember calling her and saying,

"Mom, I can move down and be close to you and do things for you when you need them."

She said, "Thank you, son, but you stay up there and get on that radio!" Then she added with a smile, "Just come visit and I'll make you some pasta." Mom was a great cook for sure.

I had not even started National Broadcasting School. It was not even a thought in my head to go to a college-level school for broadcasting. I continued thinking that some agent would come into the nightclub where I was spinning records, walk up to me and say, "Hey, great voice! Do you want to be on the radio?" This was the strategy I learned to use from the bands I worked, who played at the Troubadour, Point After, and the infamous Whiskey A Go Go back when agents were constantly out and about cruising the night clubs for talent.

I would eventually learn that no one in radio would ever come up to me just because of my unique voice to offer me a radio gig, even though some customers came up to me to request a song and say that I had a wonderful voice, a velvet voice. A radio agent just never showed up while I was spinning the vinyl. But I'm sure my mom appreciates the compliment on the "velvet voice."

The Dutiful Son

It always amazed me that when there is a death in the family, no matter where one may be in the world, they always seem to find you to give the news. My mother's death would not be the only death I would hear about within my family circle, even though I asked God Almighty to please let me get on with my life when my mom passed away, as all the previous deaths had pulled me out of time and I really wanted to get on with "life."

I think, after all my experiences, that death is a thing that just makes you stop in your tracks and deal with reality, regardless of level of success or whatever road you're currently on. When someone close to you dies, it becomes so personal that it shadows everything you try to do until you realize you have to deal with it because there is no escape no matter how busy you try to be or how hard you try to put it out of your mind. Like your index finger calling someone over towards you, it's waiting for you, and you know that you must deal with it.

My mother had left a request with the executrix to make sure that there would be no cemetery funeral and no procession of cars that would follow the hearse and the casket along the long, arduous path that would eventually lead to the cemetery. I understood this as I remember that it seemed to take forever to get my brother Richard to his place of rest.

I've spoken of my brother's death, but I never mentioned that the funeral procession not only went slowly, but it was, to say the least, torture. The mere fact that it is a group thing, people following each other, with the constant view of the hearse in front driving slowly, where the immediate family can look up from crying and out the car windshield and see the reality of what is really happening . . . it's something that must have stayed with my mom, as well as the motorcycle cops that came whizzing by from behind to the front to block traffic throughout the procession until we arrived at Richard's place of rest, Glen Haven Cemetery.

My mother wanted no part of that. Her request, according to my sister Donna, the executrix, was that no one follow the hearse from Arcadia, where mom lived just a few miles from the Santa Anita racetrack as the crow flies, all the way out to San Bernardino Cemetery, where she would be laid to rest. San Bernardino Cemetery is a military cemetery, and her second husband, my step-father, was buried there just a few years earlier since he had been a Navy man who served in World War II. He was a heavy smoker, so even though mom had quit smoking all those years ago, she would be in the living room watching TV with him, knitting, talking, and breathing in secondhand smoke.

All us kids called him Daddy Jack while they were engaged, and then when Mom married him we called him Dad, as we kids were still very young. I was about 12 and Richard was 15. My step-father was a good man—after all, my mom picked him and married him—but it was still tough on us kids, especially my little sister, Donna Marie, who is 6 years younger than me.

All that you have heard and read about divorce and children is true; it's a strain on the kids for sure. Take the custom of weekend visits with one parent and then being dropped off at the other parent's on Sunday nights. I'll just say that it's an emotional roller coaster ride. Pamela Pearl would be my half-sister once she was born from my mom and step-dad. She was the typical sassy type and grew up speaking her mind, being half Irish and half Italian, but she was my sister and I loved her just as much as my other siblings, no more and no less.

My step-dad was a strict Irish Catholic and an electrician by trade. He was one of the best. He was a perfectionist. His bosses and coworkers from Caltech (California Institute of Technology, which ran Jet Propulsion Laboratory (JPL)), commented at his church funeral that his work would stand another 50 years. I took that as a compliment, but I was pissed that day not only because my step-father, who had raised us kids since we were pre-teens, was now gone, but also by the fact that he had been just a few years away from

65 and retirement. It felt the same to me for him to be taken from us as it had when my brother died because he went suddenly.

Mom was cooking in the kitchen, and my step-dad was on the couch in the living room watching TV. I had just called my mom from Simi Valley, which is about an hour's drive.

She answered the phone and I said, "Hello, Mom, just calling to say hello."

At that moment, I could hear my mom saying to me, "Ronnie, your father is having a heart attack; I've got to go!"

I hung up and said something like "Oh, fuck!"

I left immediately and drove over to Mom's house to get directions and information on where exactly my step-dad would be at the hospital. I arrived at the hospital, and my mom was distraught over what was playing out.

She said, "Son, your father had a heart attack."

She continued to say that she was calling him for dinner and he didn't respond, so she went into the living room and realized that he was struggling to breath and had run to call for an ambulance. After she hung the phone up, it rang and it was me on the other end. That's when I drove out to my moms to get directions because there was no time for that while on the phone with mom.

I said, "I'm here now, Mom. I'm here. Can I see him?"

So while I was waiting to see my step-dad, I thought about the hell my mom had went through with her firstborn child, my brother Richard. Now, this was going down about a year after Beatle John Lennon (1940-1980) was murdered right in front of his apartment in New York, the city he loved. My stepfather was a golden glove boxer, and I remember him telling me as I got older and would visit him and Mom to watch football, "Ronnie, had I known you would grow up big and aggressive like you have, I would have trained you to fight professionally."

Light-heavy, I think he said, was the class I would have been in. I thought about how strict he had been with me and Richard, and how poor we were before he came into our lives. With all that walking I did to get to school and back, I remember having to cut cardboard to fit the bottom of my leather shoe because I'd worn a hole the size of a silver dollar in the sole. That cardboard sole would have to last until we could afford to buy another pair of shoes for me. While I had that cardboard sole, I made sure when I sat that I did not bring one leg over the other so that the bottom of my shoe could be seen. I was about ten years old, I guess. Once my mom met and married my step-dad, things got better for the whole family.

My thoughts came back to the moment when I was summoned by the nurse. I followed her down the hall to see how he was, taking a deep breath before I walked into the hospital room. There he was, lying on the bed, and I could see from his expression—at least, my interpretation of what I saw as I looked at him—that this was a setback for him.

I said, "Did you know I was here?"

He shook his head yes.

I said, "I wanted to make sure you knew I was here."

Then I left the room so others could visit with him. It was stressful for everyone, especially my mom. My step-father was, in a few days, put on life support, and my mom had to decide between unplugging the life support and continuing to hope. When I went into the intensive care unit, I could see that all his movements were from the machines. I was sure he was gone, but it was not my decision; it was my Mom's.

I think I remember that the hospital said there was no brain activity, that the machines were causing his lungs to rise and fall and if they unplugged him, he would be at rest. That stress of my mom having to make that decision, and so soon after her firstborn passing suddenly was what I think caused her so much stress that she came down with breast cancer just a couple years later. It's true that I may never know just what my mom was going through when she lost my brother Richard, but a decision was made by my mom, and my step-dad's funeral was a few days later.

There was no procession for my step-dad, just the wake at the church. Where I was living then, it was a good 3.5 hour drive (one way) to the military cemetery.

When my mom passed away a few years later, I would make that 3.5 hour drive. It seemed to take forever, and I was driving the speed limit.

Finally, I arrived and went into the office located on the cemetery property and got the info of where they'd placed Mom, and I went over to the freshly dug grave. I stood there and said my peace. I thought, *I'm here now, Mom, and now that I know you have been laid to rest, I'll return to Sacramento.* I was alone when I went to my mom's grave. No one knew I was there except the caretakers of the cemetery. Leah had already left me a year earlier on June 1st, 1984, but I went back to Sacramento and the new life that was waiting to start.

Passion of the Heart

Thinking Radio

I was starting to realize that it was not just about having a great voice and the gift of gab. I realized that I had to start to think radio. This awareness would eventually prompt me to get into broadcasting school. I had hung out at radio stations—KIIS FM in Los Angeles, for one, among others—but that would not be enough. Those indicators from when I was growing up, such as people telling me I had a great voice, especially female telephone operators whom I would talk to for lengths of time in my late teens.

My love for music was very strong, as was my passion. I was driven internally to someday work on the radio and play the hits like my favorite DJs I heard growing up and a kid. It was, to me, an exciting way to be working a job, giving prizes away and making people happy from playing their requests. I don't know if it was just trying to fill a void that drove me, but it had to most certainly be desire that fueled those 20 years!

The 20-year tenure of my radio career would only start after my mom had passed away. Mom never got to hear me on the radio, but soon after she passed away, I felt that she had something to do with my progress of getting into broadcasting school, as if she were spiritually nudging me along to get off my ass and pursue the radio career that she had urged me towards when she had said, "No, you stay up there and get on the radio."

The Vibe

I don't know where that feeling of their presence comes from when someone close to you passes on in life to the other side. I guess I'll say, for lack of another word, that what you feel is their personality, which remains even after they're gone. Soon after my brother's death, I asked a master of the arts, who also was a sculptor, just what this vibe might be.

Leo could take a square block of clay and, given a photograph or live subject, make an incredibly identical visual copy, a mirror image. He was into astral projection and practiced it, in fact. I remember him telling me many years ago, when all of us were young teenagers, that I walked like Leonardo da Vinci, which gave me pause because I always had been drawn to Leonardo's painting *The Last Supper*. Even today, I have a copy hanging in my dining room.

A lot of us back in those days gathered at the local coffee shop, mostly musicians, talking for hours and drinking coffee as if we had trained to finish our mugs just as the waitress asked, "More coffee?" I remember staying up late in those days was the norm and watching Tom Snyder's show *Tomorrow*, which came on at 1:30 in the morning, kind of like today's version of *Charlie Rose's Show* on PBS. Tom Snyder would have on his show a variety guests from all backgrounds.

So, when I called and asked Leo about sensing my brother's personality, usually very strongly, he said, "First of all, two souls cannot possess the same body."

What I was experiencing, he said, was the memory of my brother coming back to mind. But if I wanted him around, all I had to do was think about him, which he said was like a phone call to someone that's alive.

"Don't get too dependent on 'calling on him' all the time," Leo warned. "As in life, if you call someone all the time, it can get annoying."

I haven't told anyone about a dream I had of my brother Richard about a month after he was buried. In my dream, I was back on Pinyon Avenue where we grew up as kids playing Kick the Can. There was a game we neighborhood kids made up that we called Tug of Rope—not to be confused with the more generic and less entertaining version you've probably played before. Kick the Can was handed down from generation to generation, but I'm not sure if our Tug of Rope game was; maybe it just stayed in the neighborhood.

Just as it was getting dark enough that you could not see the rope (which wasn't really there), there would be a kid standing on each side of the street across from one another. When a car approached, the two kids would pretend to pick up their respective ends of a rope from off the street and pantomime pulling on the rope to block the street so that the approaching car had to stop. That's when the two kids and the rest of us watching nearby would start running towards the empty lot nearby. As we were running, we could hear the grown-up lady or angry man in the car yelling, "*Where are your parents?*"

About five houses down the block from my own lived one of the neighborhood kids, and we always hung out there and played. It was a big house. There was always food there, and his mom was like a den mother to us, making sure we ate. We broiled hamburgers all the time with lots of garlic. It was the hangout for the whole neighborhood.

There was a huge, 100-year-old Eucalyptus tree that stood next to the Dilleys' garage, and that's where we built the neighborhood tree fort, which crested the roof of the two-story house. The rest of the top of the Eucalyptus tree continued up about another 20 feet. The garage was connected to the dropdown basement, where we played Parcheesi, Monopoly, The Game of Life, and cards.

In the dream, my brother was standing at the bottom of the stairs adjacent to the Dilleys' living room, next to the entryway to the basement, and he was speaking to me. I thought it very odd that he would be in my presence because I knew intuitively (in the dream) that he was dead.

I said to my brother, "What are you doing here? You're supposed to be dead."

Richard said, "Ronnie, everybody thinks I am, but I'm not."

I never tripped on that statement. I mean, I didn't get hung up on the dream, though I thought it was kinda cool. I have always felt that Richard, though limited to our human ways of thinking, was communicating with me. What power or influence the dead have on this great earth is still unknown.

This reminds me of when I was reading the Bible and the apostles were asking Jesus what it is like on the other side. Jesus answered them, "Be busy living and don't concern yourself with that."

Me, I would be asking about electricity, but someone I had talked to over the years said to me that "it just wasn't time yet for electricity during the time of Christ." I will say this from personal experience, that sometimes some things slip through. If God is in control of everything, sometimes evil crosses our path and we must deal with it the best way we can.

I never met my mom's presence in a dream, but I do remember smelling perfume one day. I identified it intuitively, without having to figure out what I was smelling the way you have to think about a math problem. Immediately, without any thought, I knew it was Mom's perfume. Perhaps the memory of what perfume Mom wore was lodged in my mind from when I was a child. I believe that memories remain forever and, if triggered, can always be recalled.

Ironically, on the same day as the perfume smell (which was the first time I can really remember getting that smell), I got a speeding ticket. So now, if I ever catch the scent of my mom's perfume, I'm looking out for myself that whole day—and even a day or two after—in my rear view mirror.

I grew up watching Rod Serling's *The Twilight Zone* on TV, which gave its viewers another way of thinking about the paranormal, other dimensions, and things in life in general. I constantly observe how some people appear to do so much for others and planet Earth and then suddenly and sometimes tragically are gone. Rod Serling was born on Christmas Day, 1924. He was from New York. On June 28, 1975, he passed away from a heart attack. He was only 50 years old.

Graduating Broadcasting School at the Top of My Class with Honors

I attended National Broadcasting School in Sacramento. I was still thinking about my mom; it was just 3 months since she had passed away. I was watching TV and a commercial came on advertising broadcasting school, which started in a month. I turned the channel, and there it was again! I turned the channel and watched an afternoon program, and then a commercial came on and it was National Broadcasting School saying that no money was needed because a grant from the government would be available if I qualified. They also would help locate you after graduation.

I knew that I needed to get my "mind" to think radio, and I knew school would get me into that frame of mind. I went down and signed up.

They had me do some TV announcing in front of their school TV camera from a desk like a television reporter giving the 5 o'clock news. Then I did some auditioning with the microphone and some records. I talked to the director after as this was the final stage giving an interview, and then he said, "Well, Ronnie, we'll give you a call in about 5 days and let you know if you are cut out for radio."

They called, and I started school. I graduated on July 30, 1986 at the top of my class with honors, and just before graduation I was "on the air" about 30 miles away from Sacramento, in the old town of Placerville, CA. They had a nickname for that town back around the gold rush days; the ole' 49ers that panned for gold called it Hang Town because they used to hang bank robbers and cattle thieves back in the cowboy days.

Fate again played an integral part in getting me my first break into radio. I had no idea of what was coming months earlier when I was hanging around a hotel that was having a wedding reception in one of the banquet rooms that just so happened to have the doors open. I can't explain why I was drawn to the song that was coming out of that wedding reception, but almost in a trance I walked down the hall of the hotel and into the banquet room, right up to the DJ booth, to ask the DJ just who it was that was singing on that record.

He said, "It's an oldie by Tommy Edwards called 'It's All in the Game.'"

Back in 1958, the song had stayed at the top spot for 6 weeks, when I was 5 years old. It had this haunting sound that drew me to it. It was as if it was pulling me into that room, which is just one of the benefits of having been around music since before I can remember. I think if I was drilling for oil or riding the bucking bull for a living, I wouldn't have been so in tune to my surroundings and as intuitive as I am. I once met a real bull rider and shook his hand after the show, and I thought, *This is one tough son-of-a-bitch!*

I introduced myself to the DJ and said hello. It's been so many years ago that I can't remember if I gave him a tape of a show I had created in the production studio, as I'm sure I was not on the air just yet, or if a program director came to the school I was studying radio at and collected tapes we'd made, either there in school or paying money to rent a recording studio.

Somehow, this program director got a hold of a tape of a pretend show I did as if I was on the radio, the kind of make-believe game I played when I was 7 years old but this time playing the records and recording everything as it happened, such as the weather, time, news, and music information. A demo tape! The program director told me to come by the radio station and he would give me a shot, and just like that, I was on the air.

I was working 7 days a week for months before he had to cut me back a day because of the labor laws or something like that, but I was happy to be on the air! I was working the overnight shift, from 12 a.m. until 6 a.m., which gave me the opportunity to hone my skills. I was a honer, not a loner. Going from the midnight hour into the 5 a.m. hour meant that as it was approaching early morning, working folks were getting up and would hear me for at least that last hour of my show before the morning show started. It didn't feel like work to me; I was enjoying every minute.

I remember, just before I graduated from National Broadcasting School, returning to class the day after a show on real radio and having students come up to me and say, "Ronnie, we heard you last night on the radio!"

I was struck by the realization that even though I was 30 miles away from Sacramento, they instantly could hear everything I was saying and playing. It's a common thing as a jock, to get the feeling over time that no one is listening until the phone rings for a request. But that was the start of a personal awareness that even though I may be the only one in the studio, there was always someone out there in radio land listening. That's who I was talking to, that "one" person.

Before I graduated from broadcasting school, I finally asked the program director at the Placerville station KHTN 92.1 FM why he'd hired me.

"Was it my velvet voice?" I asked.

Gene Lane said, "It was because the DJ guy that did the wedding reception at the hotel had met you, and the DJ is a very good friend of mine."

People Always Ask, "How Did You Get Into Radio?"

I guess it all started back when I was 7 years old and my mother gave me an Avon microphone that came with cologne inside. I never opened it, and I still have a replica of it on a bookshelf with all the other trophies, plaques, and memorabilia I've collected along the way. I remember, in my late teens, having long conversations with telephone operators and getting comments on my voice. At that young age, I was thinking only about continuing the conversation. (I was told many times in the years ahead that I have the gift of gab.)

I didn't really get into my voice and study inflection until many years later, when I actually got into radio. I never could experience exactly what people were hearing, but it seemed that all the girls I talked with over the years, whether on the phone or in person, would comment on my voice. I'm sure when Elvis heard playbacks in the studio during a recording session with the engineers and producer, they could feel their bone marrow almost at a boil when Elvis sang "Are You Lonesome Tonight." But Elvis could never experience what his voice did to people while they listened to him sing; he could only see their reaction. He could listen to Sinatra sing and experience the emotion behind Frank's voice, but never his own.

So for me, I could only imagine what the girls were telling me about my voice. I knew "something" was going on, but that was the extent of it. I remember when I was in my early years of radio, I went to get something to eat at a Kentucky Fried Chicken and ordered my dinner through one of those ten-dollar speakers in the drive-through.

The lady in the restaurant taking my order while in the drive-thru said, "Is this Ronnie Rush?"

I thought, *Even through a 10 dollar speaker I can be recognized!*

Nikola Tesla invented the fundamentals for the radio transmission before Marconi even thought of it. Nikola Tesla is now credited with inventing modern radio; the Supreme Court overturned Marconi's patent in 1943 in favor of Tesla.

Bomb Threat

Not long after graduating from broadcasting school, I landed a job in the Central Valley just outside of Sacramento. The program director, Tom, of the 50,000 watt station KWOD 106 (pronounced *quad*), which was one of the most listened-to stations in Sacramento, had given me good advice some years earlier when I was just visiting Sacramento. He'd told me to work the outlining areas and then come into the Sacramento market to work. In other words, get some experience!

I was right on course, as far as I knew, with about a year and a half of experience out of broadcasting school. My job and experience from Hang Town (Placerville, CA) got me my next radio job at K-100, about an hour and a half north of Sacramento. K-100 (Yuba city, CA) got me the K-JOY job at the radio station in the town of Stockton, CA, known to all Californians as the Central Valley, which is a huge agricultural area.

1280am KJOY played the oldies! Program director and station manager Roy Williams gave me a break working the central valley, which opened things up for me with other radio stations up and down the dial in that area. I worked hard and studied hard even after graduating from broadcasting school. I was like a sponge, taking in everything about radio, listening to other jocks, reading books about radio and by other well-known radio jocks. I was sponge worthy! I was well on my way. I was like a locomotive at high speed, blazing a trail; I just couldn't be stopped. I was beyond driven. I was the Bullitt Train.

1280 KJOY radio had this huge picture window to look out from while the jock was on the air, and as the jock played the music and performed his show, he could see the traffic driving by, and the listeners, if they wanted, could be tuned to the station and, while sitting at the red light, turn their heads and see the jock in the window and wave hello.

After about a week of me being on the radio in Stockton, California, I was starting to settle into playing the hits. I always answered the phone and took requests, and one time the phone rang, just as it always had, and I said, "1280 KJOY. What can I play for you?"

The caller on the other end, sounding like a slime ball, said, "I wouldn't start your car if I were you!"

I took the caller seriously and called the local police, and they arrived and handled the situation while I continued to play the hits. I had learned very early on that in radio, you never reveal to the listeners what is going on, even if the building is on fire, unless it is a concern for public safety, such as a flood or some imminent disaster. The officers came inside the radio station to update me on my car, and I was told that they found nothing, which gave me some comfort. I thanked them, and they went on their way.

At the end of my shift, as I was walking to my car in near slow-motion, I got a weird feeling from just remembering the piece of garbage that had phoned the station with his idle threat while I was entertaining the city. I decided to just get in, turn the key, and see what happened. The motor turned over . . . and then started. I was relieved that it didn't blow (like in *The Godfather* movies) the way I'd been imagining it might. I was glad to be headed back home to Sacramento and to get some rest before I did it all over again tomorrow and played the hits. Oh, yeah!

Bill Graham a Well-Known Local Concert Promoter

About two decades before becoming a local concert promoter myself, by bringing famous musicians that had hits on the radio, I encountered one of concert promoter Bill Graham's concert staffers working security near the back stage area.

I was in my first decade of my radio career when I heard that Hank Williams Jr. was coming to town. His was a country act, and I'd never played country music on the air as a jock except for the one time when I left Sacramento for good (I thought) up on the border of California and Oregon. But I knew the drummer for Hank Williams Jr., Bill Marshall, from about 25 years earlier, when I had personally set up his drums as a roadie for the group he was with back then called Larry Raspberry & the Highsteppers.

Larry Raspberry, the lead singer, had had a Top 5 hit called "Keep On Dancing" with a group called The Gentrys back when I was just a teenager. Larry told me, when I had just been hired on as his group's roadie, that he'd had no more lyrics for the second half of the hit song, so the group decided to repeat the first part of the record in order to make a complete song.

When I heard that Hank Williams Jr. had arrived in town, I knew from experience as a roadie how to get backstage during the sound check. I went through Sacramento's infamous Cal Expo's Gate 12 (the backstage entrance for vehicles working the show). I was very familiar with the area, so I parked about 50 feet from the backstage trailer, as this venue was an outdoor venue owned by the city, and I walked up to the trailer and knocked on the door, asking for the road manager just as I stopped knocking. He opened the trailer door and invited me in.

I told him I was looking for Bill Marshall, the drummer for Hank Williams Jr., and he said, "Hang on a second while I call the hotel."

The hotel lobby rang his room, and then Bill was on the line. The road manager said, "Stand by for today's special guest," and he handed me the phone.

"Bill, it's me, Ronnie. I used to set up your drums 25 years ago, remember?"

Bill said, "Of course I remember you, Ronnie! Stay there and help yourself to something to eat and I'll be right over."

When he arrived, I saw him coming out of the transportation car and walked up and gave him a big hug. He still looked the same after all those years! We walked over to the rear of the stage to get up the steps that would lead us out on the stage and check out his drums.

One of Bill Graham's staffers immediately walked over and held his hand out towards me, saying, "I'm sorry, but you can't come up on stage."

Bill Marshall immediately said to the security staffer, "Hey, if Ronnie wants to come up here on stage, he can. And if Ronnie wants to sit right next to me during the show, he can. Understand?"

It seemed at that moment that all my struggles since arriving in Sacramento faded as I heard a friend I hadn't seen or heard from in over 25 years say what he said. Years later, after becoming a local promoter myself, I would say to the people working my shows, be firm but courteous.

While I was a local concert promoter in Sacramento, after retiring from radio in 2005, I was at a meeting for an upcoming concert and one person at the table said, "Ronnie, you remind me of the concert promoter Bill Graham."

Coincidentally, I had just finished reading Graham's book, *My Life, Inside Rock & Out*, which was written after his death in a helicopter crash on October 25, 1991, when he was just leaving a concert he'd promoted and was returning home in bad weather.

I said, "Well, thanks. I take that as a compliment. Have you met Bill Graham?"

He said, "Yes, I have."

"I never got the chance," I said, "but I did feel like his spirit was with me when I did my first concert in 2005."

I went on to tell him that just after I retired from radio, I thought long and hard about what I would do next in my life, and after some sleepless nights I decided to put all of my 30-plus years in the music business, from being a roadie to being a personal road manager to being a radio personality, into being a concert promoter! I decided to stay as a resident and not allow the gypsy in me to drive me from this goal.

I gave the promotion thing 100%, day and night, 7 days a week while working up that first-ever show, and about midway through the total 14 months I spent working up that show, I thought to myself, speaking to Bill Graham as if he was listening (a habit I'd picked up after I read his book), *Well, Bill, I thought this would be fun, but I see now that it's hard work. I now have an appreciation for what you must have gone through when you started out as concert promoter.*

I did have a sense that his spirit was with me while developing my first show, just as strongly as when I feel the spirit of a family member that has passed away. After all my experiences in concert promoting, my conversations always seem to include the phrase "I'm walking in the footsteps of Bill Graham" when asked about my inspiration for doing what I'm doing by bringing musical talent to the folks of Sacramento.

By the way, Bill Graham and Elvis Presley share the same birthday, January 8.

A Close Call

When I hear about a plane crash with only one survivor, I can't help but wonder why that one survived when all the rest perished. To help me understand why some people die and others are spared, I think back on that moment when Jesus told his disciples to be busy living and kept it a mystery.

We all have had close calls. I was alone when I had my experience of that "close call." I had a gypsy in me, and no matter where I was I had this drive to be on the move and traveling, going somewhere, anywhere, as long as I was on the road and in motion. I had tamed it a bit since moving to Sacramento, which I eventually came to call my adopted hometown.

As tamed as I was and could be, at the time I still would want to visit Los Angeles and some of the people dear to me. I like to travel in the late night hours as it's cooler, less stressful on the car motor, and there are very few cars on the road. So with a packed suitcase that would hold me over for a few days, I headed out to visit friends in Southern California.

I was traveling on one of the nation's most dangerous highways, according to statistics from the Department of Transportation: the infamous Highway 99. With my Class 1 license, I had driven a big rig in every state and even in Canada without any accidents, and I was now a professional driver with the experience to boot.

I was in my personal car, and I guess I had been on the road from Sacramento to Los Angeles for about three hours; I was nearing Fresno. Now, Highway 99 has two lanes going south and two lanes going north, with huge thick oleanders between them as a divider. It was about 2 am, I was deep in thought, and I was driving in the left-hand lane because it was a smoother ride in my sports car (the right-hand lane was bumpy from the 18-wheelers wearing the asphalt out).

All of a sudden, I was looking ahead of me about 3/4 of a mile and into oncoming headlights! I thought, *What the fuck is this? I'm on a southbound two-lane highway that runs one way and on the other side of the oleanders is the northbound two-lane highway that runs the other way—NORTH!*

I instinctively yielded over to the first lane and saved my own life, because that car passed me at over 100 mph on the wrong side of the highway. It was close, very close—I had about a second to move. Some asshole must have thought he was on a two-way highway and that he was in the northbound lane.

For a while after that incident, when I visited out of town I drove during the early morning until late in the day. That was really a close call. I think the transportation department should put those spikes on the off ramp like they do in parking garages so when you try to go in the wrong way your tires go flat. A life is worth more than a flat tire. I don't remember, but I could have talked about this close call on my radio show when I returned back to Sacramento.

About 5 Years After Broadcasting School

Radio is divided into markets: New York is #1, Los Angeles is #2, Chicago is #3, San Francisco is #4, and so on. If you are wondering about the K and the W at the beginning of the radio station's call letters, it denotes the regions divided by the mighty Mississippi river. The east side of the river is W, as in WNBC. The west side of the river is K, as in KNBC. Between 1986 and 1990, after I had busted ass in the Central Valley, Merced, Modesto, and Stockton, working every little station up and down the dial, I got a break at the #2 station in Sacramento's radio market #27, the 50,000 watt KWOD 106.

It was supposed to be pronounced *quad*, but I remember one jock on the air said the call letters just as they appeared. While on the air, for all of Sacramento and the outlining areas to hear, Pat the morning guy said "K–wad 106."

The station manager ran all the way down the hall, and you could hear him even from the sales office yelling, "You say 'K-wad' one more fucking time and you're FIRED!"

I think Pat said it again while the owner was listening, because he was gone from the morning show soon after.

KWOD 106, at its peak, enabled jocks to transfer from the Sacramento market to the Los Angeles market with ease because the station was well respected by other programmers in the country.

I was very lucky to be working at this Sacramento radio station where the #1 program director happened to have been hired on from Los Angeles' legendary 93 KHJ radio. Gerry Cagle was Los Angeles' PD at the height of the Boss Jock era in the 70s.

My "in" to KWOD 106 radio was through the sales department, going out and about to all the businesses in Sacramento. Since I researched Cow

Town in my early years with Fran's advertising company, I knew before arriving at the station that Sacramento was a "testing" ground for new companies and the products they sold, ranging from grocery outlets to Mom & Pop stores to all retail and on and on. This knowledge gave me an edge among my peers. I knew that as I drove around town, when I saw a Grand Opening sign or Under New Management, my reflexes were trained to react!

I would park my car and get out, and as I was walking up the front entrance of their business I would be calculating what I saw and writing their commercial in my mind. I worked hard for months, always wearing a suit and tie, always hustling to get ahead of my associates, of which there were about 8, sometimes 10. We all had to be at work by 8:30 a.m. and back by 5:00 p.m. to report on our day.

One day, after months of being with the station, we all gathered in the sales room, which had a big, long corporate table where all the sales staff sat with the sales manager, John, at the head. Program director and station manager Gerry Cagle's office was just down the hall, and he would pass by sometimes while we were in sales meeting and look right at me and smile through the glass.

The sales manager at the head of the table said he had an announcement: "Ronnie Rush is now the #1 salesman among us!"

That continued into the following month as well, and then into the third month following. That's when Gerry Cagle called me into his office and said, "Ronnie Rush, you are on the air tomorrow morning 6 a.m. Good luck, enjoy your show, and don't forget to record your show and have your air check on my desk first thing Monday morning."

I was ecstatic. Going on the elevator from the 22nd floor down to the lobby, it seemed like I was floating. I remember Danny Hamilton telling me years earlier that in a dream he'd had, I was wearing a suit and tie overlooking the city from the top floor. I was as ready as a track star at the Olympics waiting for the gun to sound at the starting line. My opportunity to break into the Sacramento market was here. No fear, Ronnie Rush has arrived!

I made sure I was awake and ready that Saturday morning for the first time I was to be on the air in my adopted hometown of Sacramento. Yeah! Oh, sure I could be heard in Sacramento while I worked the outlining areas of Sacramento. While you were cruising in your car, though, you would have to manually move the radio dial to tune me in. When scanning for a Sacramento radio station in Sacramento, the scan would only pick up the heaviest Sacramento signal. Now, anyone pushing the scanning button in Sacramento would find me.

The show went great, and I listened to the air check many times and made a copy for Mr. Cagle. The following Monday, I was back in the sales office where I still worked, thinking to myself that Gerry Cagle, former PD of the legendary 93KHJ Los Angeles—where the great Robert W. Morgan, the Real Don Steele, Machine Gun Kelly, worked—now had the tape on his desk from my first Sacramento show in market #27.

Then Gerry Cagle called me into his office.

He said, "Nice haircut, Ronnie. Go ahead and have a seat."

I sat down, just busting at the seams wondering what he was going to say about the show that I'd done a couple days earlier on Saturday morning.

Gerry Cagle said, "Ronnie, I hired and fired Machine Gun Kelly."

He had my undivided attention.

Gerry said, "I was listening to your show Saturday morning."

I said, "You were up at 6 a.m.?"

"Ronnie," he said, "I listen to the station twenty-four-seven."

Gerry went on to give me a life-changing piece of advice regarding my career in radio. He said, "Oldies."

He explained it to me this way:

"Ronnie, when you and I are talking here, you are one way. Then, as soon as you go on the air, your delivery and mindset is oldies."

It made sense to me as he said it. I had grown up listening to the Real Don Steele, Robert W. Morgan, and the Big Kahuna on Los Angeles' big hit-maker, 93 KHJ radio—though when 93 KHJ was playing the hits of The Beatles, the Rolling Stones, The Who, and Sonny & Cher, they weren't oldies yet; they were newly released records. I now had a direction. I could finally head on and pave the way for my future radio career.

Gerry stood up, shook my hand, and gave me a copy of his book, on which he'd written "To: Ronnie Rush, read this and you'll know how it's done in the big time! Signed, Gerry Cagle." His novel is called *Payola!*.

Point to Ponder

There have been many movies made in Hollywood to portray just about every kind of situation that can arise for mankind except about a radio DJ. Finally, Howard Stern put out a book that became a hit movie in 1997, directed by Betty Thomas. *Private Parts* portrays what it's like for a real radio jock coming up the ranks of radio. Thank you, Howard Stern, for bringing attention to the radio DJ.

Hands of the roadie, keeping a grip

The Limo Company, 1988

As I look back over the many, many years of being here in Cow Town (Sacramento) since my arrival on March 4th, 1984, the thing I remember most is taking clients through the famous Old Sacramento—especially tourists, as we had a lot of those—then letting them out to walk along the Capitol building.

I showed off my city to clients like the great host I was, taking them around town to the nightclub scene and to see the sights just up the road a couple hours in Reno and Tahoe. There are many great restaurants as well, and everyone loved seeing the night lights overlooking the world-famous San Francisco Bay.

Heading into San Francisco at night, I always heard the clients in the back of the limo *ooh*ing and *aah*ing as they looked out the window at the historical Bay Bridge. The San Francisco Oakland Bay Bridge is a toll bridge that spans the San Francisco Bay and links the Californian cities of Oakland and San Francisco. Then we traveled further down and made the turn to drive over the historical wonder of the Golden Gate Bridge, known to everyone all over the world.

With the help of my job, I became very familiar and comfortable with my newly adopted hometown, Sacramento. Being a limousine chauffer gave me the opportunity to make my way, not only through making some money but also by letting me meet people and make new friends along the way.

The story of how I even got into the limo business is that fate thing again working its magic in ways that can only be seen years later as I look back. In fact, some of the things that I look back on that came together for me seem to be out of my control, the direction of a higher power I'll call God.

I've wondered sometimes why God waits until the very last minute before he steps in. It was 1988, and I had no idea that the job I had at the Sacramento Hilton would open the door for the job that would propel me into gaining more knowledge about my newly adopted hometown.

I was hired on as disc jockey by an older Hotel manager who wanted to hear oldies music during the happy hour. I was working radio and club gigs to bring in revenue. The whole hopeful idea was that as the evening rolled on, the hotel guests would come down and be joined by the Sac town locals, and I would start playing dance music. The more they danced, the more they would drink and the more the cash register would show that things were picking up, which gave me some job security.

But as the days went on, there were not enough people at happy hour and then at the evening's playing of dance music to support the manager's idea of having a live disc jockey spin records while they drank down their spirits, ate, and danced. So the manager cut my hours down to just happy hour, and I knew my days were numbered.

I think that by this time I had already auditioned for several nightclubs, as the competition was stiff at the more popular places like Stuart Anderson's. I was part of that competition, coming in second of the 50 or more club DJs that wanted that one position. A real cattle call.

But that fate thing, which was unknown to me at the time, was unfolding. During one of my last happy hour sessions, I was behind the DJ booth and looking around at the Hilton bar area when I saw for the first time in a long time two customers. They'd come in the side entrance and sat at the bar and were carrying on a conversation with my only true loyal listener for much of the time, the Hilton bartender.

So I put on a song and walked over to say hello to the two customers and to grab a 7-Up.

One of the guys introduced himself as Glen and said to me, "Hey, I guess we're your only customers."

I said, "Hey, how are you guys? I'm Ronnie, and you're right, you two are my only customers in a long while."

Glen said, "This is my general manager, Jeff." Then Glen said to me, "Ronnie, have you ever driven a limo before?"

I said, "Well, I've driven cross-country and I have a class 1 license."

Glen said, "Ronnie, if you want a job, my office is just behind this building we are in right now, and right by the pool is my office. Come by and I'll show you around."

My life took another major turn and I became a limo driver just a few hours after that moment. I was on the move again, sort of, making money and still pursuing my radio career! The gypsy in me was fading, and my roots were digging ever deeper into my adopted hometown.

Still to this day, 23 years after that meeting, I'm friends with Glen and Anita, Glen's wife. Early on, they would invite me over for dinner, and their kids became like nieces and nephews. Glen called me one day out of the blue some years later while I was working on the air here in Sacramento; I was locked into the radio gig by that time.

Glen said, "Ronnie, I'm building a new house in El Dorado Hills and I don't trust anyone to run my company. I need to be on site everyday while they build. Would you come and run my company?"

I said, "Glen, I finally got another radio gig and I'm finally back on the radio." I explained to him that it's really tough to get on any station, even on weekends.

"But yes," I said, "I'll run your company for you."

That house Glen built was the very house where I meet Joe Esposito, Elvis' friend and road manager and Glen's new neighbor.

Six degrees of separation

Rush Limbaugh

I drove a limo to support myself while I was pursuing my radio career, and one day I was waiting in a tuxedo for my clients to come out of Mace's Restaurant. I remember standing close by him out in front of Mace's in Sacramento. He was alone, just standing there, and when I realized that it was Rush Limbaugh, I walked up to him and said hello. He was just in from New York visiting.

Rush was kind to me, and he remembered that I had sent him a thank you card years earlier, for taking time out of his busy schedule to give me advice, as he was not only the top announcer on Sacramento's air waves, but his station KFBK talk radio, was consistently in the #1 top spot. I had just graduated from National broadcasting school in 1986 and was on the radio, working the outlining areas of Sacramento. I never saw Rush again.

Mayor Sonny Bono

By the time the late 80s rolled around, I had worked every position in radio and had reached one of the short-term goals that I set after graduating broadcasting school: landing in Sacramento's radio market #27. I had been working as a limo driver to make money while I pursued the radio career Gerry Cagle had advised: playing oldies. So I worked at getting on a radio station that played oldies or something close to that format.

Gerry Cagle's station was alternative music, but it was great experience and I took that experience and his advice and applied it to the next level, which would be any oldies station up and down the radio dial in the Central valley or Sacramento. While working on that, I kept working the limo gig to pay the bills.

One time, I received a call to take Mayor Sonny Bono over to McClellan Air Force base and drop him off at the officers club for a speech he was going to make. Then I would return him back to his original pickup point. He was a true gentleman. While driving him, I thought about his and Cher's huge 1965 #1 hit song "I Got You Babe," which always reminded me of my hometown Sunland-Tujunga.

I have very pleasant memories of meeting him and of the reminiscing that song brings as well. I was sad to hear that Mr. Bono passed away at 62 years old in a skiing accident at Heavenly Resort in southern Lake Tahoe while on vacation with his family in 1998. Sonny had been a frequent skier at the slope for more than 20 years, the resort said.

Super Freak Rick James

I once got a call to pick up Mr. Rick James and take him over to the Sacramento Memorial Auditorium. I pulled up to the Hyatt hotel downtown and the manager for Mr. Rick James said before I could get out and walk to the rear door, "We got it."

Then they got in on their own and we were off. As we were headed over to the venue, the manager said to me by way of the intercom phone, "Ronnie, let's head over to Dr. Smith."

Rick was not feeling well, so the manager asked that I take him to get a B-12 shot. We headed over to the facility where the doctor was waiting and again the manager said, "We got it."

They got out on their own, and since the rear door of the limo was parallel to the doctor's office front door, it was just a few steps before they were in the building. Since it was a Sunday, I could park anywhere I wanted, so I stayed right where I was by the front door and waited. (There is a lot of waiting in the limo business.) I got caught up on some of my paperwork, and about a half hour later, Rick James and his manager were in the car before I knew it.

I looked through my rearview mirror and could see that the private partition of the limo and the glass partition were down, and the manager said, "Ronnie, let's head to the venue."

I drove down I Street to 15th & J and pulled up to the back door of Memorial Auditorium. There was a pause, and then from the back of the limo the manager said, "Let's wait a few minutes until Rick is ready."

I could actually hear his voice just as if I were sitting across from him at a dining room table because the private partition and glass partition were still down. As I waited for word from the back of the limo, I had time to think about seeing Rick James in those MTV and VH1 videos and to think about the nightclubs I had worked in as a DJ playing those music videos so the crowd could get up and dance to his funky music. I remember looking at the videos and seeing Rick up on one of the seven big screens the nightclub had mounted all around for everyone's viewing.

Then I heard Rick James say, "Ronnie, I'm ready."

I got out, walked to the back door of the limo, and opened the door, and as Rick "Super Freak" James got out, I was surprised to see that he was not as tall as I thought he was. I'm 5 feet and 7 inches, and Rick was a couple inches shorter than me. So now I see why people would say when they meet those artists and actors that are up on the big screen, "Wow, I thought you were taller!" Even for myself in radio, when I would show up to do a live remote broadcast around town, people that listened to my show got an opportunity to come up and say hello and would say, "Oh, Ronnie Rush, I thought you had blond hair and blue eyes" or "I thought you had brown hair and were taller."

Whether it is the big screen or the radio, listeners' imaginations produce their perceptions. There is a phrase in radio that we jocks say to one another when we meet after talking on the phone for the first time that goes, "We never look the way we sound." So true. We call it the theater of the mind! When a female caller would ask, "Ronnie, do you have blond hair?" I would say "Maybe," allowing them to keep the theater of their mind going. Let the listeners imagine whatever they want lets them enjoy the music more. But for those of you who are imagining what I looked like while on the air, you should know that for most of my radio shows, I stood.

Paula Abdul

Paula Abdul was on tour around the time of her big 1988 hit "Straight Up" while I was picking up some clients in the limousine backstage in the tunnel of the famous Arco Arena, home of the Sacramento Kings. I found a spot to hang out easily because there were very few vehicles backstage except those who have a special backstage pass. The tunnel led to the back area where I was parked, which is just a stone's throw from the stage, the very stage on which Paula Abdul had just finished performing.

After parking, I got out of the limo to stretch my legs and wait for my clients, who were somehow connected to the promoter as guests. As I was looking at the huge tour bus in front of me and thinking about my days on tour as a roadie, I looked to my left and there was Paula Abdul.

She was only a few feet away from me in my tuxedo, as most chauffeurs wear to concerts, New Year's Eve parties, and so on except for funerals and Napa Valley wine tours. A coat and tie are worn for funerals, and during the summer the chauffeur can dress down their shirts and shoes, and if the legs got a whistle from the ladies, it was okay to wear short dress pants just above the knee. I was looking at Paula, and I could immediately see that she was exhausted from her show. She seemed to be taking it in—the experience, if you will, of her surroundings, the Arco Arena backstage area, or maybe she was just in deep thought. I noticed that her tour bus was full of people, and it seemed as though she would be the last one to board the bus.

I wanted to say something to Paula, but I knew she was exhausted and decided to not engage in a hello. My role at that moment was chauffeur, so I held back. Just standing there for those few moments was a nice memory for me, however. I imagine when I was on tour as a roadie there were those kids that got close but never got the chance to say hello. They probably have some pleasant memories also.

Time is Ticking

Leah's father, after his triple bypass heart surgery around 1991, hunted high and low for me like a private detective and discovered where I was working. I found out later that he also was driving a limo, and if you and someone you know were both driving limos in Sacramento you eventually would run into them because of the concerts and events always going on around town. People wanted a designated driver while they partied to avoid DUIs and high fines and possible jail time.

I was general manager of this limo company; I had worked my way up the corporate ladder over the years while pursuing my radio career. I started as a greenhorn hired just for airport runs and had worked all the way up to the front office. Now I drove when my special clients would call, like the casino crowd gamblers or Napa Valley runs or to see the night lights of the San Francisco Bay. I had my choice of any of the charters that came in as part of the agreement signed when I was promoted from chauffeur to GM of Glen's limousine company.

All of this was accomplished since that moment when Glen was my only customer while I was spinning records at the Hilton hotel and his office was behind the hotel, when he offered me a driving job. Like I said at the beginning of this book, never give up, never give up, never give up!

This was around the same time Joe Frank called me to say that Jerry (the guitarist that played with his teeth) had committed suicide. Jerry was like a step-brother to me, and I miss him. I only wish he would have tried to contact me because there is always a way out, always. But when you kill yourself, that one last opportunity is gone forever. I'm reminded of him and his brother who played bass and Boogie who played drums when I promote a local show, and I can't help but think of how great it would be to have them open the show for a national artist.

The last time I heard from Jerry (one of the greatest guitarists unknown to the world) was when he called me to say that his mom had passed away. I told Jerry that I too had recently lost my mom also, but somehow it was not enough for him to reflect to move forward, as I knew when I was his roadie that him and his mom Agnes were very close.

About 6 ½ years after Leah and I were no longer an item, Leah's dad showed up at my limo office door.

He said, "Ronnie, can I have a word with you?"

Can you imagine what I was thinking? Here was Leah's dad asking if he could talk with me. The last thing he said to me years ago, about putting a restraining order on me if I didn't stop calling, was burned in my memory. The very people I had considered future in-laws had cut all ties without explanation.

I want to say that there was never, ever any violence or harsh words to her parents during the breakup or towards Leah, for that matter. I loved them all like I loved my blood family; he was just being a dad and doing what dads do when the daughters change their minds about who they are dating. I think I even remember something about how it's a woman's prerogative to change their mind. I've heard men say, "Life is not easy." I don't know if this was said just after a woman changed her mind with them, but I've heard it said a lot and know it to be true that life is not easy, and all the guys say Amen!

I said to Leah's dad, "Yes, sure, of course. What's up?"

We went outside. I was in my mid-thirties, and he said, "Ron, I want to apologize for what happened with you and Leah." He continued, "That was me that got in between you and Leah."

I said "Okay."

Then I shook his hand and he walked over to his nice new car and drove off. I had somehow heard about his triple bypass surgery maybe a year before, but I called a nurse at the hospital and told her what had just happened.

The nurse said to me "People that have triple bypasses have a life expectancy of about 5 years."

I serendipitously ran into Leah at my bank (Great Western, now Chase) a few years before her father showed up at my limo office while I was in the long line at the bank. I happened to look up ahead three or four people and noticed a redhead, and when she turned in my direction I said, "Leah, is that you?"

It was her. Leah looked awesome; the last time I saw her she was just a girl one year out of her teens, and now she was a young woman of about 27. I was not lost for words, but I could hardly believe that she was just a few feet away from me. I was glad that circumstance had brought us to the same point in time, and I knew she knew that I was not trying to follow her (not that I ever did).

So I casually said, remaining in my place in line, "What brings you here?"

She said, "I'm getting a divorce and I'm cashing a check."

I thought to myself, *Wow, she got married.* Then it was her turn to move to a teller. The line I was in moved slowly forward, and she finished her transaction and then left. It was the strangest coincidence; I had a whole list of errands to do and only at the last minute did I decide to turn into the bank when I did.

After her father met up with me at the limo office to apologize, I initiated a call. Again, this was a couple of years after running into her at the bank and about 7 ½ years since we broke up. Somehow, I found her number. It had been so many years since my conversation with her when I told her that I would wait for her and she replied, back on June 1, 1984, "Ronnie, you'll be wasting your life!"

I took a deep breath, exhaled, and dialed the number.

The phone rang, and then Leah answered, "Hello?"

I said, "Leah, this is Ronnie. Hi. Your dad just stopped by my work and said that he was sorry and that he was the one that got between us."

Leah said, "No, he didn't!"

I said, "Whatever. Goodbye."

Then I gently hung up the phone because I never would say any harsh word to her because she had been my best friend earlier in my life. I still have some great memories and no one could take them from me. Alzheimer's, maybe, but no one else.

Like Mom said, I was a gypsy. I had traveled all over the country and was always on the move. One thing Leah did for me was give me roots.

Voice of the roadie

Sacramento's Oldies Radio Station Cool 101.1fm 1997

It took about eleven years of focus and hard work to finally make it "officially" into the Sacramento radio market #27 from the time when I graduated from broadcasting school in 1986. I remember, just 4 years after graduating from broadcasting school, when program director Gerry Cagle of the legendary 93 KHJ in Hollywood had transferred to Sacramento, gave me the advice early on that oldies should be my focus, which put me on the right track. Thank you, Gerry Cagle, and now it was finally getting ready to pay off.

One of the top program directors of a popular oldies station in Sacramento who was still functioning in radio during my tenure of radio was Jon Brent. Like Tommy Lasorda was to the Dodgers as a players' coach, there was Jon Brent, a jock's PD. Jon Brent being on the west coast at the same time as myself created an opportunity for me to finally lock into the Sacramento radio market. He was a very entertaining afternoon drive jock; his high ratings showed that, as did him bringing the station into the top 3 of all the stations on the dial in the Sacramento market.

I was about to become part of that success. Over the years I spent as a radio personality, I would make a copy of my shows and drop them off at every radio station where I wanted to work that played music with a bit of personality. Just to intro a song and give the time and temperature was monotonous to me, but if they hired me, while I was there, I would take that opportunity and time to hone my craft while working my way up to the larger radio markets.

Back before computers did all the work playing the music and commercials, we jocks had to pull the next hour of commercials and music and place them in their appropriate sequence and time to play for that hour. There was no computer. You put a commercial in the slot and a song in another. If the log called for three commercials, then you would pull from your stack and place three in individual slots on standby, then jingle after the last commercial and into music. This was all done by the jock. When I went to an interview, the program directors would comment about how tightly I ran the board, which is a huge compliment. The women program directors usually complimented my voice as well, and I would tell them, "My mom appreciates that I'm sure. Thank you!"

John Brent had listened to my air check from a station I worked at in the Central Valley, B-93 in Modesto, and asked me to come in and talk. I was a bit nervous because this was not only a major station but it was one located in my adopted town. Working the airwaves came natural to me, and in all the years leading up to this moment of my interview, I had become a polished radio personality. Wax on, wax off, baby!

I sat down with him, and he went over the issues regarding the dos and don'ts of radio. I gave him my info for the Human Resources department and got my schedule. I was the happiest person there at the Cool 101.1 radio station. There were four stations under the same roof, and when they held their company party, 500 people showed up for the Village People's concert at the Red Lion Inn banquet room.

One of the stations, KFBK, coming in at #1 during every Arbitron ratings poll, was an all-talk radio station in Sacramento which, just a decade ago, had had Rush Limbaugh at the helm. I walked the very halls where Rush Limbaugh had walked.

I arrived for my first shift at Cool 101.1, and in my jock mailbox was a realization of a personal goal I set for myself after graduating broadcasting school and an indicator that I had finally officially arrived in radio: a Top of the Hour I.D. that said (*quick music intro and drum beat*), "And now, ladies and gentlemen, Ronnie Rush on Sacramento's oldies station COOL 101!"

A few days later, a "Jock Shout" arrived in my mailbox, and I popped that in the control room board cassette player, and as the song ended, I hit the PLAY button. Out came a chorus of female singers in harmony singing, "Ronnie Rush! Cool101!"

Over a period of time, I stopped being a diamond in the rough. Top radio programmer Jon Brent had taught me the art of radio, and I had become a pro.

And on Mother's Day, I kicked off a song, opened the mic, and said, "Mom, your son is on the radio!"

Princess Diana

I was on the air at Cool 101.1 on August 31, 1997, when I heard about Princess Diana's car crash with her close companion Dodi Fayed. Once it was verified that she was dead, I pulled one of the music carts out of the files that read "Love is Blue." I made the announcement after I pushed the play button. French orchestra leader Paul Mauriat's # 1 song "Love is Blue" stayed at #1 for 5 weeks in 1968.

MKB

I decided not to use the real name or a pseudonym of the person I'm getting ready to mention here, but I will put his initials. I met MKB through some friends that golfed in Rancho Marietta, a place where MKB actually lived on the Country Club golf course with other homes that grazed the sidelines of that 18-hole golf course.

This was a really nice, upscale place to golf; you not only needed a pass to get through the front gate, but to golf, you also needed to be with a resident who was a member. The residents there were able to go out of their front doors and into their garages, hop into their private golf carts, and head down to tee off on the first hole. That's what I call style!

MKB was one of the top criminal defense attorneys in Sacramento. Our first meeting was pretty forgettable; I knew this girl and she needed a ride to court, so I gave her a ride and MKB was her attorney. After the court hearing, this friend of mine introduced me to MKB. I shook his hand, and then he was gone, though I met him again a few years later on the golf course.

I remember seeing him on TV, as he was usually doing high-profile cases. One reporter asked MKB a question on camera during a live newscast about a current court case as he stepped outside the courthouse, and MKB said, "That so-and-so has been a pimple on my ass!" MKB reminded me of that movie star James Cagney to a tee (no pun on the golf thing intended).

MKB became like a brother to me over time as I would run errands for him and his wife Cindy when I wasn't on the radio or driving a limo. Cindy would pack a brown bag lunch with a bunch of goodies for me to make sure I had something to eat while on the air in the Central Valley. A couple years down the road, MKB and I were having lunch at David Berkley's, located at the Pavilion Center, which always reminded me of an area in Beverly Hills.

Incidentally, Mace's restaurant was just a few doors down from where I had spoken with Rush Limbaugh years earlier.

Anyway, we were having lunch on the outdoor patio, where there were many outdoor tables being used by other patrons. All of a sudden, this shady character of a guy who owned two limos of a company I used to run walked up to our table and made an accusation about a stereo or VCR in one of the limos being gone, trying to say I had them.

Suddenly and without warning—and I mean quicker than a karate stance—MKB had pushed his chair back and was right in the face of the guy that was accusing me (this is where that James Cagney profile came to me).

MKB said, "Look, pal, if you got anything to say to Ronnie, you say it to me!"

The guy said, with his lip snarled up, "Who are you?"

MKB said, "I'm his attorney."

The guy walked away.

I never did like that feeling of being accused of something that I didn't do, but I've noticed on this road of life that there are some people along the way that are blind to the truth. For some reason, MKB knew from the get-go that I was as honest as the day is long! Again there was that familiar feeling that came over me when my brother Richard did the very thing MKB had just done. It was comforting to know that I still had great memories of my brother Richard even so many years after he had left this earth. Over the years since, there have only been a handful of people I've met that have been able to bring back such comfort, who have made me recognize that they also see in me what my brother Richard saw and treasured.

One day, while working on the air at the Sacramento radio station Cool 101.1 (which I always thought had a great radio signal on that frequency), I went into the Fax/API room, which receives information from all over the world of American Press International. There also was a fax machine, and coming through the fax machine was a message that read "Ronnie Rush #1 voice in radio!"

Later, I was able to get the original, and I still have it to this day. Thanks, MKB.

It was about this time I quit smoking cigarettes, on February 1, 1999. There is no drug in the world that compares to being on the air. It's a natural high. It's the best feeling I've ever had.

~Radio~ A Letter to Jon Brent

From the very beginning of my radio career, when I graduated from National Broadcasting School in Sacramento, I told myself that one of my goals was to be in a top 5 radio market within 20 years. I was so excited, I wanted to tell Jon Brent, one of northern California's top program directors, who had taught me the "art" of radio, that, beyond my dreams, all my talents had brought me to the level of am 610 KFRC radio in San Francisco and that I'd been hired on by program director Bob Harlow. I was scheduled for weekends with the idea for me to syndicate my show eventually across the country. He told me this while I was handing him my driver's license and other documents to copy and file for the company's HR department.

I remember renting a new Mustang convertible and driving from Sacramento to San Francisco, thinking along the way that this was finally the big break in radio that I had worked so hard for over the years. The reality was setting in as I was paying the toll fee for the Bay Bridge and was just about nearing my destination.

Then I was there, pulling up to the KFRC building for my 1:30 p.m. appointment. I finally parked, only to be told by the guard in the building that the entrance for KFRC was around the building. I drove around and found a parking spot right out front with still enough time to make my appointment with the program director of the #4 station in the US market. I remember thinking, as I walked the short distance from my rental car to the entrance, that my past experience of always being on time and always being prepared, had gotten me through even to that moment.

I went into the door the guard had pointed me towards earlier, but when I stepped into the lobby I found that the heavy glass doors in front of me were locked. I thought, *I'm going to be late!* Then, at that very thought, an elevator door to my left opened. The afternoon jock I had been listening to on the way into the bay area was standing there and he said, "Hey there!"

I said, "I'm looking for KFRC radio and I think I'm going to be late for my appointment."

He said, "This is the back entrance, and this is the freight elevator, I was going to smoke a cigarette but come on I'll take you up."

As we were going up, I was so relieved. It was like being rescued. I still to this day can't remember the conversation I had with the afternoon jock—this was my big moment!—but you can bet I was relieved and grateful for sure. We walked out of the elevator and into the KFRC office area, passing by a line of cubicles and finally making it to the reception area, where I was asked to wait for Mr. Bob Harlow.

When Bob Harlow came out of his office, we shook hands and he gave me a tour of the company, the few studios they had and the production studio before we returned to his small office. Bob Harlow started telling me his plans for me, how he wanted my radio show to be syndicated across the country from the bay area. But after about 20 minutes, I said to him, "I think the meter is going to expire and I don't want to get a ticket."

Bob reached behind his desk to get a handful of quarters and said, "Let's go down and put a few quarters in the meter."

So there I was, walking down the streets of San Francisco with the program director of KFRC! It was surely a great moment for me and a memory I'll never forget.

Point to Ponder

I realized there was creativity going on while I was on the air live, and one day what came out of my mouth was this statement: "Life goes on when you pass on, but it's more devastating when you're still alive and life passes you by." After all the years since I was with Danny Hamilton recording that music he was creating live in front of my eyes at the quadruplex my father owned, I personally got to experience firsthand just what he may have been tapping into. Besides moving tape carts around and pushing buttons and answering the request lines, my personal experience with that "source" is that I felt "plugged in" to a power of some kind. The best way I can put it into words would be to say that as I was talking up the ramp of the song, I felt my "being" connecting to some universal source.

Retiring from Radio After 20 Years

Looking back on my years on the radio and thinking about some memorable times, I never have any trouble recalling a conversation I had with one female caller. I was working the 7 p.m. to midnight shift and answered a call.

"Hello, Cool 101!"

The female caller said that she was listening to my show right now and she had gone to bed and all the lights were out and she was relaxing under the covers while she listened to my show.

I said, "Can I play a song for you?"

She said, "No, Ronnie, but your voice is turning me on. I want you to keep talking to me."

I said that I would play a song for her and dedicate it to a friend. "What is your friend's name?"

She said, "Just play something and dedicate it to me."

There is a fine line that I would walk many times as female listeners called or showed up at the back door of the radio station after a shift or when I was doing a live remote, personal appearance somewhere in the city. My experience as roadie and doing the radio thing was, for me, two different worlds. I kept the ladies from my radio days at an arm's distance and the ladies from my days as a roadie in my arms.

I always wondered how a football quarterback knows when it's time to pass the torch to the next up and coming player. I watched the great Joe Montana, quarterback for the San Francisco 49ers from the early 80s until he retired. Joe Montana always worked magic on the field, especially in the last 2 minutes of a game. Some announcers called him the greatest quarterback of all time. Hearing announcers during the games say "Montana to Rice" over and over all during his prime years become part of pop culture.

But all things have a way of coming to an end. Joe Montana retired from the game of football. I always said to my friends, "Now that Joe Montana has done it all, breaking lifelong records and actually playing for another team against his own team and beating them twice, he should now coach the 49ers." What a day that would be for the fans as well as the up and coming rookie quarterback that would be mentored by the greatest quarterback of all time, Joe Montana.

I remember back in 1975, H, JF&R were playing the Santa Monica Civic, and The Grass Roots with Rob Grill opened the show. Alan Dennison was friends with radio personality MG Kelly from Los Angeles' 93 KHJ radio, and as a one-time favor to the group he came out and announced the group. I was asked to announce The Grass Roots, and this was 10 years before I was even thinking about radio.

I went out there and said, "You've waited a million years and cried a billion tears, but you don't have to wait anymore. Ladies and gentlemen, The Grass Roots!" Then MG Kelly went out and announced the group H, JF&R and came over to where I was sitting stage right.

I thought, *Shit, I'm sitting next to the #1 jock from 93 KHJ's powerhouse radio station in Los Angeles, MG Kelly!* Life is funny that way. I remembered listening to MG Kelly growing up and then there he was sitting right next to me.

Years after the time I announced The Grass Roots, 10 years to be exact, MG Kelly listened to air checks from radio shows I was doing early on in my radio career and critiqued them and gave me some pointers. I actually still have a recorded message he left. I don't know if I ever told anyone about MG Kelly mentoring me, as I didn't want to come off as being someone special over my other radio peers. I kept it to myself. I just wanted to hone my craft and become as good as I could be with what I had to work with. I remember how nice those radio people were when I was on tour with Hamilton, Joe Frank & Reynolds. Coming into town with a #1 record on the charts, the DJs treated us like kings!

MG Kelly, the great Robert W. Morgan, and the Real Don Steele were the exceptions to the rule of when I learned after actually getting into radio and being a part of radio culture was a rude awakening. The radio DJs that I thought were just the greatest things since baked bread were nowhere to be found. Most were ego-driven, self-centered, and selfish. I had to adjust quickly and realize that I was not only on my own, but I would not get any advice from the jocks along the way during my tenure in radio. I was lucky to have MG Kelly to send my tapes to about every 5 years for critiques while working the mic. The other radio basics I had to study and learn on my own, but I learned fast. I have a knack for learning things quickly. My brother Richard had a photographic memory. Richard could read a page of movie script and, after setting it down, recite word for word what he'd just read.

I made some goals for myself during broadcasting school. One of the short-term goals was to get into the Sacramento market. Another goal was to be in the top 5 radio market within 20 years. An ultimate goal was to sit in for Casey Kasem. Though having my feet on the ground and reaching for the stars (as Casey Kasem would say at the end of his Top 40 countdown), I never got to sit in as a guest DJ on Casey Kasem's American Top 40 countdown.

Many years later, I would email Dick Clark because of his *Rock, Roll & Remember* radio program. He emailed me back, saying, *Thanks so much, Ronnie, for sending along the mp3 of your radio show. I enjoyed listening to it. At this time, I don't believe we can be of any assistance to you. Please rest assured, however, that we'll be sure to keep you in mind for the future. Sincerely, Dick Clark.*

It was nice to hear back from Dick Clark; I wanted to see if I could sit in as a guest DJ, like Casey Kasem would allow once in a while with his countdown show, *American Top 40*. Even after retiring from radio, I still get the itch to apply once in awhile to a radio station. Even program directors I worked for in the past would write in support of me. One such PD wrote, *"Ronnie worked part time as a weekend/fill-in for me toward the end of my tenure when I programmed COOL 101.1 in SAC from 1993 to 98. At the time, we had created a 'boss radio' Oldies persona for COOL 101.1 and Ronnie delivered as I asked. He took direction well, followed our plan, and his passion for radio and music translated well on air and I was happy to have him on my team,-* Jon Brent program director." There is one thing I want to mention since retiring from radio and that is I'm glad I was able to pay off my student loan!

Point to Ponder

I can't help but look back some 25 years or so and vividly see some parallels to myself while I was itching with ambition, just starting out and trying to make it big in the music business.

There was Jay Leno, whom I saw standing with the stewardesses near the cockpit of an airplane back in 1975 as Hamilton, Joe Frank & Reynolds got off the plane. I remember looking up as I got near the front of the plane to exit and seeing the familiar face of a young, dark-haired Jay Leno as he was just starting out.

Another person on the rise was Rush Limbaugh, radio announcer. When I first arrived (to visit) in Sacramento in 1982 or 1983, I remember Rush debating the mayor of Davis on a local Sacramento television station, KCRA TV 3. Years later, in 1997, I landed a job on Cool 101.1FM radio, where I walked down the very halls of Chancellor broadcasting (now Clear Channel), where Rush was propelled to national stardom from Sacramento's KFBK's AM all-talk radio.

Even Oprah Winfrey started her career at about the same time I started my radio career. She, born January 29, 1954, and I, born December 2, 1953, are the same age, within a month.

Even with my short-term goals met, while striving for some long-term goals, I wondered a lot why I never was able to make it to their level of success. I was not really in a race with them; it's just that we all started out about the same time. As Mick Jagger said in an interview, *"You can work hard, have all the talent in the world, and good timing, but it takes a little luck to make it."*

Making a Wish

All of us have come across a situation where we wished for a certain thing to happen that we hoped would be for the good and benefit of ourselves. After I retired from the radio, I pursued the idea of announcing for the PBS television station since everyone over the years of my radio career had said I had a velvet voice, a radio voice. When I spoke to someone on the phone, they would ask, "Are we on the air?"

So, I tried to contact my favorite voiceover person, Will Lyman, from the TV program *Frontline* that airs every week (Will also did the BMW commercial that aired constantly in those days). Of all the many voices I've heard over the years (and because I have no idea of what my own voice sounds like) I personally think that Mr. Will Lyman is the best ever!

Besides having worked up and down the radio dial, I had worked every aspect of radio. When I sit down and watch a TV program and hear the narration in whatever it is I'm watching, if I like the narrator's voice then I stick to the article and hang to watch the program. I've heard Sigourney Weaver, Stacey Keach, Morgan Freeman, and others, but for Will Lyman I stopped in my tracks to watch as he narrated the program.

When the lead singer's voice is appealing, it tends to make the rest of the song come together. An example of that would be the lead singer of the super group Journey, Steve Perry. He is no longer with the group Journey (at this writing) but Journey the group continues to tour without Steve Perry, as the group found a tribute band that played Journey's music and hired the tribute band's lead singer to sing Steve Perry's songs. I cringe when I think about how it's possible that an unknown singer could step into the shoes of Steve Perry and sing all of Steve Perry's hits and tour while people paid the big bucks to go see them play.

I'll tell you a conversation I had recently as a concert promoter with one of the booking agents I was negotiating with to bring an artist to one of the venues here in Sacramento.

I said to Bobby (the agent), "I want the original singer!"

Bobby replied, "Ronnie, people don't give a crap about whether or not the original lead singer is on stage, they just want to hear the fucking music!"

With all my years of being not only alive but in the music business, I find it offensive that anyone would pay big bucks to hear a band just because the band name is well known and there is only one original member remaining and not even the original lead singer that "made" those hits on the charts. Yes the music is a great part of the whole, along with the original singer, but to years later bring in an act to perform a slew of hits from that band after, say, 30 years of radio airplay and not have at least it's original singer, is to me a close second to a tribute band.

I'm referring only to the second level groups, not the Rolling Stones. Can you imagine having the Rolling Stones without Mick Jagger? Let me say it this way: For me, having the original "sound" of a group perform is worth the ticket price paid. If I cannot get close to the original sound that was heard on the radio, then I will look for the next artist that is. But people are paying to see acts that have no original members because the years gone by created this void due to either break-up or death.

I'll say it does work for some groups of the past, but in my eyes, very rarely.

Anyway, so I wrote PBS to see if there was a way to reach Mr. Will Lyman so I could ask how he got into doing the narration thing. No luck what-so-ever! I went online and found nothing. I wished that I could just ask how he got into doing narration, how he prepares when he's reading the script for *Frontline*, or if he had written a book so I could read it.

About a year later, that private wish I had made came true. Being persistent during that year paid off. I was browsing online and stumbled across Will Lyman's website! Voila! I clicked on the email from his website and Will Lyman himself replied. I told him who I was and about my radio background and that I watched *Frontline* because of his voice, which I told him that of all the narrators was my favorite to listen to. I told him that because I was told I had a great radio voice, I wanted to check into doing narration for television, as I thought one of the key things was the *voice* that made people stop and watch the program all the way through, the way it does for me. I even sent him a copy of my radio air check. He wrote me back, and here is what Mr. Lyman said:

RR - Your voice is pleasant, friendly and accessible. Clearly, you're good at what you're doing here. Hard to tell from this whether it would be good in doc narration because of the style of the medium the sample was taken from. How well do you sight-read? A good test is answering this question: Can you make sense of material whose words you don't understand and make the read fluent and smooth? Can you back the "first person" quality out of your material, blend into the background?

Personally, I don't think it's the VOICE as much as the simple conveyance of information. Can you read so that we are aware that you are a sentient human being without feeling as if you required us to have the same response as you to what you were saying? Just off the top of my head. WL[1]

---

[1] The fact that Mr. Lyman took the time to write me back, gave me inspiration to continue my journey in researching narration as a possible position where I could apply my voice. The mere fact of "knowing" how narration is conducted, gave me perspective. Self determination, that I was able to eventually find a contact that I thought highly of, in the field of narration.

Alan Dennison Reunion

During the years at the helm of my radio career, I kept in touch with Danny Hamilton and his wife Fredricka, as I had always considered them family. Danny, Joe Frank, and Alan had long ago broken up. I always wondered why musicians struggle for years and years, make it, and then turn on a dime and break up. I never understood why that happens, but there are many theories to explain this madness. I have just accepted the fact that Hamilton, Joe Frank & Reynolds was no longer.

Alan Dennison, from what I remember of the breakup of the group, moved back east to New Jersey with his new wife and worked a day job for many, many years. It was thirty years, in fact, before I would ever see him again in person, and it would happen when I was going to the 610 KFRC radio station in San Francisco to meet with the program director, Bob Harlow, that would end up hiring me the very day I saw Alan Dennison. I was so excited to have accomplished the long-term goal of being in the top 5 radio market within 20 years of graduating from National Broadcasting School with top honors.

Then, as I left the radio station, I was going to see Alan Dennison, who was just a few miles away from KFRC radio. I pulled up to his apartment, parked, walked up the narrow outdoor stairs that led to the top floor and knocked on the door. He came to the door and it was him for sure: Alan Dennison, the greatest piano player I've ever known and worked for.

He invited me in, and we sat in the living room, which had a lot of windows with natural light coming into the living room at about 1:30 in the afternoon. I was amazed at how he had aged. I even said, "Alan, you've aged!"

He said, "Yeah, it happens."

It always amazes me when people see a movie or television star they haven't seen in years. They always say, "Wow, they have really aged!" Why is it that we don't see ourselves age the way we do others?

We talked about the past and what he was doing currently, and I told him that I had landed the gig at the #4 radio station in the country. Time passed, and then it was time to go. I said my goodbyes, and as I hugged him, I was thinking about how much hell he had gone through during his heart surgery, the same kind endured by Governor Arnold Schwarzenegger.

I said to him, "You're the greatest piano player in the whole world."

He walked me down to the bottom of the stairs, and we spent some more precious moments together as he mapped out a way for me to catch the freeway back to Sacramento.

If you get a chance, besides listening to the *Fallin' in Love* album, there is a song off the *Love and Conversation* album that Alan Dennison wrote while living across the street from the famous mansion of the magician Houdini (March 24, 1874—October 31, 1926) and wrote the song. I think it's a trip that Houdini passed away on Halloween.

Joe Frank Reunion

I think I was already on the radio and had achieved some moderate success when I drove down to Hollywood where Joe Frank lived. In his spare time, one of Joe's passions was photography. He was an assistant to the lead photographer for *Playboy* magazine, owned by Hugh Hefner, who also owned the record company Playboy Records, for which H, JF&R was the first group to give Hugh Hefner a top of the charts number one gold record.

As I was driving down from Sacramento, I had time to think about the years that had passed. I remember calling Joe one time and saying to Joe Frank, "Joe, that one *Playboy* model is really beautiful. Can you introduce me to her?"

Joe Frank replied, "Ronnie, you and a million other guys think the same way."

I thought about a lot of things while I drove from Sacramento, and then I was there in Hollywood, pulling up to Joe Frank's house. I walked up the long driveway and knocked on the front door, and there was Joe Frank. He looked like he always did, tall with long blond hair and just as kind as always.

I walked in and sat down, and we started to talk about old times. It was great to be in Hollywood again. It's the energy I'm referring to; if you've ever been in Hollywood, even just to visit, you would know what I mean, but to live in Hollywood, you would really get hooked.

Joe Frank always showed me love like a brother, no matter how many fuck-ups I did when I was younger. He must have understood that it was part of not only growing up, but life. I remember a time when Joe Frank and I lived only about 10 blocks from the ocean and the roads to the ocean were flat, Joe Frank let me use his 10-speed bicycle. There I was one day, riding down Santa Monica Boulevard, the main road to the ocean, not a care in the world and thinking about the girls and the white sandy beach and the scenery when all of a sudden—and I mean within an instant—I was flipped into the air, did a double summersault (great for the swimming pool), and slammed to the ground with the force of a body slam!

I wasn't wearing a helmet—no one did back in 1972—but I got lucky and did not kill myself or land on my head. I got up, brushed myself off, and then, to my surprise, found that I would not make it to the beach, as close as I was, because the front wheel was totally warped, so warped that I had to pick the front end of the bike up as I walked all the way back with the rear wheel rolling to Joe's place. The front wheel had caught in an iron drainage ditch grill, which was just wide enough for the front wheel of a 10-speed bike to slip through. I was lucky that day. I had a paper route as a kid, and I don't remember any drainage grills along the road nearest the curb. Boy, the rich have just about everything—even drains!

Joe Frank was much older than me, but I had early on stayed with Joe when I first started working for H, JF&R. Living in west L.A. near the ocean was a totally different atmosphere from living inland. One evening after a Disneyland gig, as Joe Frank was dropping me off at my brother's house in Tujunga, where I was staying, Joe said to me, "Ronnie, pack your stuff up and you can come and stay with me."

I remember being just blocks from the ocean, where Joe Frank lived. The ocean gave the area an atmosphere of openness, and the people as well were open and friendly. It's a special place for sure. This was about the time Looking Glass had the #1 song "Brandy (You're a Fine Girl)" (1972).

Hamilton, Joe Frank & Reynolds (back when it was Tommy Reynolds in the band) was just finishing up a 2-week stint playing at the famous Tomorrowland Terrace in Disneyland. The stage rises from underground and eventually becomes level with the audience that is anxiously waiting for the show to begin.

Down in the dressing room, just before show time, Tommy Reynolds would tell stories about when he lived in the village back east, where he witnessed Jimi Hendrix getting kicked out of a night club for playing too heavy. Joe Frank told a story about a show they did in Japan where, after the curtain had just opened, someone from the audience jumped up on stage in a karate stance in front of Joe Frank. Danny Hamilton walked over from center stage, removed the man with his own brand of karate, then walked up to the microphone and said, "Good evening, ladies and gentlemen. We're Hamilton, Joe Frank & Reynolds."

With just a few days left at the Disneyland gig, my brother Richard and his wife Connie came out and got to see firsthand my work and the concert. We all got a package of tickets to go on some of the rides on our time off. I surely was one to enjoy this part of the job. I went on the ride I think was called "The Shrinking Machine." You got on the ride, and as you went through a tunnel, everything around you shrunk. Then, when the ride was over, you went back to normal size.

It's been a while since I was there, but I remember that when I got off the ride and was headed back to the Tomorrowland Terrace for the next show, I reached for my wallet in my back pocket and found it was gone! I quickly ran back to the ride I had just gotten off and asked the employees there if anyone had turned in my wallet, which had my free Disney ticket package, $80 in cash, and my driver's license. Nope. No one returned the wallet, even when I checked back after the H, JF&R show.

To this day, I carry my wallet in my front pocket. I later was thinking that when I shrank, it must have popped out of my pants. Probably not, but I always thought about when I was on that ride, The Shrinking Machine, that that's when I must have lost my wallet.

[Authors note; I always thought that when Joe Frank played his bass guitar that he had the same feel as Beatle bass player Paul McCartney. The harmony of Joe Frank, Dan, and Tommy (and later, Alan) was a great blend. My favorite song was "Annabella," and Joe Frank did an awesome job on that and shared the lead with Danny. Oops! Now everyone knows my favorite song.]

A Guitar Pick and T-shirt

Danny Hamilton, lead singer, songwriter, and guitar player for Hamilton, Joe Frank & Reynolds (and now my best friend) has an incredible voice, and I can only compare it to maybe Elvis Presley or Engelbert Humperdinck or maybe even B.J. Thomas. I had early on asked Danny if he would consider doing a remake of "He Ain't Heavy He's My Brother" by The Hollies, which was #7 in 1970. He shook his head and said no.

I always thought Joe Frank would do a great job if he were to remake the Sanford/Townsend Band's hit "Smoke from a Distant Fire" (#9, 1977). Even today, when I hear that song I can actually hear Joe Frank as if it was him singing it. That's how close that song is to the way Joe sounds. I know many people have their own favorite singers, but Danny Hamilton is one of my favorites. His singing captured you, as you can hear in his ballads, which also captured the hearts of the ladies when he was live in concert. Roses would just appear on stage. Fans would walk up to the base of the stage and leave gifts for the musicians in the band. I think I heard Joe Frank say one time that he heard that they were called the "love" group by one of those newsstand magazines.

I remember Alan Dennison and I were once sitting in his apartment, which overlooked the ocean, having coffee with a little amaretto liquor for flavor.

He said to me, "Ronnie, you are our number one fan."

I said, "I love you guys with everything and would continue to work hard to make things on the road as easy as possible."

He acknowledged that I was their Super Trouper and told me he made sure that the title "Ronnie, Our Super Trouper" would be on the *Love and Conversation* album, which also would have all three of their names on the front cover. (If you can find that album, you'll notice there are barcodes on the album, which came out years before the grocery stores were using them for pricing.)

Soon after the album's release, the group would be no more, but I remember things to this day that tell me it was not because of the music they wrote and performed in front millions of fans. It was something beyond my comprehension at the time.

I kept in touch with Danny over the years, sometimes even driving down to see him. When I was not visiting him, Danny would be on the other end of the phone playing live, with his acoustic guitar, a song he'd just written. Once in a while he would play a song that was just about finished from the recording studio he was using somewhere on the Sunset Strip in Hollywood. He would ask me what I thought and I would tell him, "Damn, Danny, that's a top 10 hit for sure!"

Danny was not feeling well; he told me a month before Christmas of 1994 that he would be going into the Cedars-Sinai hospital for an operation and that it would be a big ordeal for him, as this operation was a critical one to his health. He told me he loved me.

I said, "Yes, I know."

He said "Really, I love you, Ronnie." And this was serious stuff going on.

"I love you too, man," I said.

Danny said that if he made it through this operation he wanted to get the group back together.

I said, "Awesome. I'm excited Danny, really excited." I asked, "Danny have I made it to road manager?"

"Yes," he said.

I also asked Danny if this was worse than anything he'd been through.

"Yes, Ronnie. More than anything I have ever been through."

In late 1994, he went into the hospital for his operation. He told me that the first 24 hours after the operation were critical, but after that would be a good sign of recovery. Danny made it through the operation and was sent home, I believe, 7 days later.

That Christmas, I started to call some of the close people in my life. When it came to calling Hamilton, Joe Frank, & Reynolds/Dennison, I called Joe Frank first.

When I called Joe Frank on December 24, 1994, Joe's wife answered the phone and I said "Hey! Merry Christmas! Is Joe Frank there? I want to wish him a very Merry Christmas."

Joe's wife said, "Haven't you heard?"

I said, "Heard what?"

Mrs. Joe Frank Carollo said, "Ronnie, Danny Hamilton passed away last night."

Point to Ponder

Danny had gone to one of those well-respected psychics in Hollywood. Danny told me the psychic read his chart, which paralleled John Lennon of the Beatles and Elvis Presley, the king of rock and roll. Another twist I see as I look back is that they all died while in their 40s.

Epilogue

About a week after Danny passed away on December 23, 1994, his widow Fredricka asked me if I wanted to follow the casket on the plane to Spokane, Washington. I said no. I didn't make it to the funeral either. I just could not believe that Dan was gone.

Years passed, and it took a toll on me as the toxins built up inside from putting off facing the death of my friend. When Joe Frank's wife told me the news of his death, right then and there I knew it was all over for good. I'd thought we all had a chance to come back, as everyone was still alive and I knew Dan had written some hits; he'd played some of them on the phone for me over the years and prior to his death. I was still working on the radio at STAR 100.9, Superstars of the 70's. I would always give Danny a plug since a lot of his songs were from the 70s and we played them in radio format, and I liked to give little bits and pieces the public never knew from behind the scenes. For example; *(radio bit coming out of a song)* "Star 100.9 that's Hamilton, Joe Frank & Reynolds, with their # 1 Gold record, Fallin' in Love, and that's Joe Frank's cousin on drums. It's 4:25 with Ronnie Rush… traffic next!"

I drove down to Los Angeles where Fredricka lived to visit and connect with her about a year or so after Dan passed. We talked about old times and the guitar of Dan's she was giving to a Hard Rock Café type of club to put up on their wall. I stayed the night in the living room, and the next morning we had breakfast and went through some pictures.

It was good that I got to see Fredricka after so many years. My heart wanted to stay with her and live nearby so I could be around should she need anything. Just as with my mom, I wanted to move down from Sacramento so I could be close to be available, but the reality was that we all have a road in life; sometimes they cross paths and we are able to enjoy those times. Other times, we must take the road we are given and pursue what is up ahead for us as an individual. But if Fredricka ever needed me, I was just a phone call away.

Of all those hundreds of pictures, I found one that I liked of Danny sitting in his living room, turning slightly toward the camera, and to this day it's in a nice gold frame on top of my refrigerator because Dan and I always talked a lot in the kitchen. I guess Dan wanted the living room clear of any negative energy, and we had some heavy conversations at times, in the kitchen.

Dan had some insecurities, but I was too young to analyze them. Back around the time of the Burbank House, I had been in contact with Casey Kasem's secretary, trying to get information on how to fulfill my goal of filling in for Casey as a guest DJ. It was long ago, but I remember telling Danny that Nancy Conover, Casey's secretary, said she would do a "Whatever happened to Hamilton, Joe Frank & Reynolds," and if Danny wanted, Casey Kasem could mention he was working on his solo album. When I showed Danny the letter from Nancy Conover, Dan blew a gasket! I was still a young kid in his eyes (I was in my 20s), and he told me to not get involved in his business. My desire to help Danny get the kind of exposure he could have used to promote his solo career stalled out.

I remember when we went to Playboy Records on Sunset Boulevard in Hollywood. Barbi Benton, Hugh Hefner's girlfriend at the time, wanted to sing and record a song, so a record company was created called Playboy Records. Dan had dropped his demo tape of "Fallin' in Love" off at every record company along Sunset Boulevard and was turned down. But because of Barbi Benton and the timing of that new record company, Dan dropped off the demo tape of "Fallin' in Love" and was given a thumbs-up! After a lot of studio work, the song was released and climbed the charts to the top spot, to #1. Another twist of fate was on the horizon. One of the female executives for Playboy Records would eventually become Danny's wife. Her name was Fredricka.

The song was either climbing the charts or had reached #1 and was dropping that day when we got off on the seventh floor, and I waited in the lobby while Danny went in to talk with some of the record executives. A few minutes later, while I was skimming through a magazine (no, not Playboy), I could hear Danny yell, "You're taking food out of my daughter's mouth!"

Yep, he was pissed off. He came out and we went back to the elevator. I pushed the button for the first floor. If there was an ASAP button, I would have pushed that too!

The doors closed. I said nothing.

Then Danny said, gently, "You want to go and get something to eat at Twains Restaurant?"

He would often have outbursts of rage. Where it came from, I can only guess; it was probably leftover energy from the concerts because I've experienced the audience energy during a show and it's like cannon fire, but in a good way. I didn't think too much on the outbursts, as I had more or less figured it wasn't about me anyway.

There was that one time when Roger the truck driver was hanging at my quadruplex for a 24-hour period before I hit the road with him. I was antsy because I needed to be moving and on the road, in motion! Roger left the house to run an errand, and Dan came in with a baseball bat and swung it in front of me, hitting the kitchen cabinets.

It's a good thing my reflexes were there; otherwise, I would have been hit. Dan was pissed about something, or maybe it was all in his mind because Roger was built like Lou Ferrigno of *The Incredible Hulk*. Dan's conscience may have bothered him about his outbursts over the years, and I think he was worried that Roger would confront him about his behavior. Dan didn't know Roger but for a brief introduction when Dan had once happened to drop by. Roger was an intimidating presence, but for the ladies, he was adored by them. So having Roger confront Dan was the furthest thing from my mind, and I would never think that Dan needed an ass-whipping from Roger.

About a year into being on the road with Roger, he and I were in a bar having some beers and playing pool. I was not aware of this, but Roger went over to two guys that were hanging around me and said, "If you guys are looking for trouble, you are going to have to deal with me."

The two drinkers hanging with me said, "No, we're just hanging around."

Roger said, "Well, I've been watching you two guys, and I'm asking you to lighten up on Ronnie and take your friend to another bar . . . now!"

Roger was looking out for me as I was mourning my brother Richard, but each day that went by I got stronger.

Like I said, I didn't hear from Alan Dennison for almost 30 years. I don't know why I always had to initiate on my end to make contact, but I did. For instance, when he lived in San Francisco for a very short time, I saw Alan the very day KFRC radio hired me. That was God bringing together something that I could never have arranged because just after that meeting with Alan, he moved east to Virginia.

Alan made an odd comment when I arrived half an hour early. He said, "Hey, I thought you were going to be here at 2 p.m., not 1:30."

Even after 30 years, he made that comment. Maybe I took it wrong; maybe he meant it was a pleasant surprise to see me sooner. I don't know because I never asked, but I got the impression that I was cramping his style by arriving 30 minutes early, which was actually not bad on my part since I had timed everything out from Sacramento early on. But all in all, as they say, it really was great that I got to see Alan in person and give him that hug and say he was the greatest piano player in the world. That meant a lot to me to be able to tell him in person those very words from my heart.

Ten years after Dan's death, I thought it better for me to finally go to his grave site, which is up near Seattle, Washington. It took me about a year, while still battling to get back on the radio, to save up the money for flight, hotel, rental car, food, and so on. I called Dan's brother, Judd Hamilton, and told him that I wanted to fly up and asked if he would assist me in finding the cemetery where Dan was laid to rest.

Judd said, "Sure, Ronnie. It's about a 5 hour drive from Seattle."

So after getting everything ready to go (from Sacramento), I knew deep down inside of me that this would be one of the best things for me to do as I remembered the years leading up to this moment. I carried so much tension after his death that at times, when a friend would come up from behind me and put their hand on my shoulder, I flinched. I knew that I needed to do this, as stressful as it was to stop what I was doing in Sacramento and to feel the trauma coming over me at the very thought of flying up to the gravesite of my friend Danny Hamilton.

What I would do when I saw his tombstone? Would I cry? Would I be able to hold up even though almost 10 years had passed since I'd heard he died on the operating table at Cedars-Sinai hospital?

I drove my car to Sacramento International Airport and parked in the 7-day area since the other choice was overnight. I boarded the plane that would bring me closer to my destination, the cemetery where my best friend Danny Hamilton was laid to rest.

Airports now are making people take their shoes off? I look forward to the day when our airports are back to where they were; that surely will be a good sign that we are able to move freely again. Yes, some jobs will be lost, but we must get back that which we lost before the snake took a bite of our freedoms. God bless America!

I arrived at Sea-Tac Airport, grabbed my luggage, rented a car, and headed to the hotel to check in. I took a deep breath, and then I called Judd and told him I had just arrived and was on my way.

It was just a few miles from the hotel over to Judd's government-assisted housing apartment. We met, and then we were on our way. I could see that Judd had aged quite a bit since I had last seen him. We had talked over the years by telephone, but to see him in person showed me that time was moving forward. No matter how many memories we keep in our minds, frozen in time, life moves on.

There was a heavy rain, but going over the summit to Spokane, I knew that the 4-wheel drive I'd rented from Sea-Tac airport would get us over just fine if it were to turn into a light snow.

It was a long drive, so we stopped to eat. While Judd was gulping his food, I was thinking about the time that had passed since Joe Frank's wife told me Dan passed away. For me, I was just about to experience another tragic moment in my life. The thought that I was just an hour from walking up to the gravesite of my friend Dan was starting to overwhelm me as I remembered how much he had endured in the year before he passed away. But I was ready to face what was ahead.

Judd was still eating like he hadn't eaten in a few days. I was glad to be here in the moment and to have Judd, whom I had not seen in 25 years, with me while I approached the cemetery and eventually the grave. If I did break down and fall on the grave after 10 years of holding back, I figured Judd would comfort me. After all, this was Dan's brother.

Judd ordered desert, and by the time he finished I was ready to get on the road. I paid the bill, and then we were back on the road. As we arrived at the cemetery I started to get that familiar feeling that I'd had previously when arriving at a cemetery, and I thought I might cry because it was a long, long time since Danny had died.

Judd and I walked along, and as we got closer and closer to the grave site, he seemed to remember the area. Then he said, "Wait a minute. I know he's here somewhere."

The snow on the ground had not totally covered the grass or the headstones of the cemetery, and he soon found Dan's grave. I realized as soon as I saw Dan's name and the actual grave that it was not only real but final. Danny was no longer on the earth.

Judd commented as we stood over Danny's grave, "Ronnie, it's almost 10 years to the day, and you are here for the very first time."

He'd said before, a few miles before we reached the cemetery, "Now, Ronnie, we Hamilton's don't cry." I thought that to be very insensitive. So I stood there over Daniel Robert Hamilton's grave, and after a moment I squatted down and ran my hand and fingertips over his full name on the tombstone. Then I was ready to leave. It was very stressful for me. Judd had been there 10 years ago, and I'm sure those raw feelings had had time to heal. But for me, as I walked away, I was in the zone.

On the drive back in my rented car, Judd wanted to stop and see his other brother John, whom he said was ill, but all I wanted to do was get back over the summit before a heavy snow closed the roads! I was in no frame of mind to socialize, even though I knew John. I just wanted to get back to Seattle, because it was a little longer of a drive than Judd had said it would be just going one way.

Judd bitched about my wanting to continue on, bringing up some negative crap from years ago, but I stood my ground and since I was driving, I said we're not stopping. My memory of him from many years ago was of a kind, gentle, and compassionate soul, but he was not the kind, gentle host I thought he would be.

When we arrived back in Seattle, I dropped Judd off at his apartment and said, "I'll come by in the morning and we'll have breakfast."

Then I drove the few miles back to the hotel. I can't remember how I was feeling, only that I was looking forward to spending time with Danny's brother. The next morning I went over to see Judd for breakfast, thinking we would go to the famous original Starbucks for coffee. That did not happen.

Judd said, "I want you to go."

"Huh?"

Judd said, "Ronnie, just leave. I don't want to see you. I want you gone."

I was stunned. I walked from the living room through the hall to the opened door of the bathroom where he was shaving and said, "You want me to just leave?"

"I wanted to play a song for you that I just wrote," he said.

Then I said, "Great. Let's go get some breakfast then come back."

"No," he said. "Just leave."

I walked out the front door, and when I turned around he was at the front door and said to me, "You were Dan's friend anyway."

Then he shut the door.

I stood there for a second or two, thinking he would open the door and say he was kidding or something like that, but he didn't; the door remained closed. I could not believe that Judd was acting this way. I knew he was bitter that his brother was gone, but I too had lost a brother, and I knew immediately from the sound of the door shutting that I was not wanted.

I waited out my couple days at the hotel to return back home to Sacramento, and the thought that I had a home to go to was comforting. As I boarded the plane and took my seat, I reflected back on the beginning of my trip. When the plane reached the altitude where the stewardess said we could release our seatbelts, I was glad to be going home. I accomplished my goal, as stressful as it was, and the year it took for me to scrape and save the money to fulfill that goal was worth it.

While I was looking out the window thinking, I thought back to times when Judd would visit at the Burbank house. Judd and Danny had gotten into some knocked out, dragged out fights over the years. They never touched one another, but they had very brutal arguments just inches away from each other's face. To this day, I've told no one about my private trip to visit the gravesite of my friend Dan. No one but Judd knows I made the effort to do so.

The moral of the story is that no matter what you do in this life for others, no matter how loyal you are to others, it all comes down to one person, *you!* Be good to yourself.

Ciao, Ronnie Rush.

Danny Hamilton

It has now been almost two decades since my best friend Danny Hamilton passed away. The road has always been rough for me, even while Danny was alive and even way after the group broke up. I somehow always felt that the group would return to the recording studio and, with Danny's voice and writing ability and Alan and Joe Frank's talents, they would produce another hit. Those days at the Burbank house were an incredible space of time, and as I look back on those days I really am glad I have those memories.

Dan was a volatile human being. Just being in his presence you could feel the incredible energy that surrounded him. It wasn't really a force field energy; it was an energy he would send out, and if you were close within range I would describe it as another type of force of nature, like the wind.

We had become close like brothers. I remember him telling me after I relocated to Sacramento, "Ronnie, what are you doing up there where all the cows are?"

To this day I can't remember what I said to him, but I think my destiny at that time was to continue pursuing my radio career and those goals I had set for myself. I really think about that time at the Burbank house when Danny, the singer, songwriter, and guitar player told me those words of comfort, "Ronnie, don't you worry. When we play the Salt Palace, that will show her! "

So now I have to believe that things would have worked out, that Hamilton, Joe Frank & Reynolds would be on tour and I would be the road manager as I had strived to be so many years ago.

Afterword

I decided to write this chapter to bring some light to the perception of contacting someone that you know that has made the Big Time. I have found that each person, no matter what the skill, must blaze their trail to success on their own. There seems to be a perception that if someone close to you has "made it," hooking up to their train will allow you to follow right behind them, as their road to success now is wide open to them. But I have come to realize that just because they are successful, it does not mean that their success can be shared. Each person who makes it big is really a single success with no room for any other up-and-coming talented whatever it is that the world will maybe soon come to know about them.

For some reason, all during my tenure in radio, there was always a human being that determined whether or not I got a break. Generally speaking, these people that give you a break are total strangers to you, yet they have the power to decide whether or not your world will be about you bringing out the best in you so your talent (whatever it may be) can be shared with the world.

I'll give one example. Joe Frank, bass player for the group I was fortunate to work for, received numerous tapes from people he knew over the years that played music or were in bands and asked Joe to listen to and critique them. The critique part is okay, but for Joe to give that person a break just would not be as easy as it seems just because the light of success was upon Joe. You have to trail your own path, which is not an easy thing to do because it takes determination, perseverance, hard work, and skill just to get to a level where you can present yourself as a talent that has not only potential but the "right stuff." Having the "right stuff" blazes the trail for you, and at that time, as the smoke from that trail is seen, you then will draw attention to yourself and then the human being that notices that smoke will give you a shot at the big time.

So there is a process to success. Like the baker that kneads the dough, work your craft so that when an opportunity does arrive, you will have a shot to present just what it is you've got. Be ready.

Point to ponder

If only there was a way to go back in time! Turning the clocks back one hour is not enough. Maybe someday, someone will figure out how to step in that time machine and visit other eras. A professor once said that if you could build a receiver sensitive enough, you could pick up President Abraham Lincoln's speech because it's still out there in the air! President Abraham Lincoln and Thomas Jefferson are my favorite past presidents, with the warrior mindset of Andrew Jackson, our 7th president, at a close third.

Radio

Now, retired from radio, I see that radio has totally changed. Computers have reduced the need for a live, on-air jock to a minimum of hours per day, leaving more money for the shareholders of the corporate radio stations that own much of the stations, from the small market radio stations to the larger markets in each town and big cities across the USA. Maybe it's a monopoly that has taken over in radio; maybe the big machine just doesn't want to run 24-hour radio with local professionals in each small town or large city, even though that puts fully qualified people out of work because most of the frequencies up and down the radio dial are now owned by a handful of corporations that have created a lockout in favor of the massive radio stations they own across the country that would have allowed thousands of radio personalities to have work. Bill Moyers and others have talked about this subject on the PBS network television stations across the country.

In the earlier days of radio, most of the radio stations up and down the dial were owned by individual owners who employed a staff to fill the 24/7 shifts. There were all live jocks 24 hours a day 7 days a week all across the USA. If it did not work out at one station, a DJ could just go down the dial and work for another local owner or fly or drive to another town and work there.

Once the computer was designed so that the memory could handle the commercials and then, later, the music, it was just a matter of time before the live jock was phased out. The mega corporations now own most of the stations in the country due to deregulation in 1994. Before, only one AM and FM station could be owned by a company in any given market. Then President Clinton signed a bill that allowed corporations to buy up as many as they wanted in each market across the country.

What I'm doing today as I write my memoir is concerts. My passion is still burning inside me to succeed in whatever it is I'm doing in the music world. Even after all the zig-zagging I have done over the years since the very beginning of my arrival in Sacramento, I still feel as strongly about pushing forward and making a go of my new direction as I follow in the footsteps of one of the top concert promoters, Bill Graham presents.

I don't know, if I was offered work today in radio in another major city, that I would even attempt to move, because the gypsy in me is back in the bottle . . . for now.

The love of my mom from all her years has stayed with me to this day. Yes, a mother's love is everlasting, a special gift she leaves for all her children.

About the Author

Ronnie Rush started his journey in the music business long ago. At the early age of 2 he started to get the gift of gab. Then at the age of 10, he started to think of a radio name. Ronnie's influences came from radio and the personalities that were blowing through the radio speakers, in the early 60's. Such talents as The Great Robert W. Morgan and The Real Don Steele, Ronnie's favorite jock of all time.

Growing up in Southern California had some great opportunities for Ronnie. Living near Malibu beach to enjoy and weekends in the mountains, and venturing out all over the valley as time passed. As a teenager, Ronnie's interest in music grew, especially when Ed Sullivan introduced to the world, The Beatles! I was hooked he said, after hearing, "I want to hold your hand." It was a smash hit! #1 and I knew then music was for me. He continues to say; that there seemed to be a feel for picking a hit record. I had a knack for picking a hit & telling where Casey Kasem would land it on the Top 40 Countdown.

Soon, in his late teens, Ronnie was meeting musicians and got an offer to be a roadie. As soon as a year or so had passed the group Ronnie worked for had got an offer to be the front band and tour with such acts as the Drifters and Shirelles . What an experience! He said, Wow here I am on tour and meeting all these great musicians I was listening to as a kid on the radio. Ronnie was then introduced to, Hamilton, Joe Frank & Reynolds. They needed a roadie to go on tour with them and of course he accepted. Life changed at that moment. Now, the level of musicians Ronnie was meeting, all had hits in the current top 40 Billboard magazine. Even on tour we had time to stop and see a concert. There I was walking back stage with HJF&R to meet Karen & Richard Carpenter. Their band called The Carpenters. Then it was off to Chet Huntley's Ranch in Bozeman Montana to do a benefit concert. At the resort we all got our own bungalow cabin. By the time we did the show we were having a meal with such stars as, The Skipper from Gilligan's Island. Miss Donna Douglas of the Beverly Hillbillies, sat right next to me while we ate. Wow, there at the end of the table was Joey Heatherton (she did the SERTA mattress commercial) This all was around the mid 70's.

Ronnie continues to say, even checking into the Holiday Inn you could turn around and see other artist hanging around waiting to get a room. Such artists like Seals & Crofts Boz Scaggs to mention a few. Those were the days!

After the group broke up I decided to get into radio. I was in Sacramento, CA when I attended National Broadcasting School. I graduated at the top of my class with honors, and outstanding achievements in the year 1985. 20 years I dedicated my life to the radio gig. Since radio changed (in my view) that live jocks 24/7 across the USA were no longer needed, I decided to change careers. In 2005 I did my first concert as promoter.

I do know one thing is for sure, nothing comes to anyone easy. You have to work hard and even harder to get over that hump that will eventually welcome the arrival of all your hard work. I see now just how hard it must have been for promoter Bill Graham, when he started out. So my advise to all who get an opportunity to read this is 3 things. Never give up, Never give up, Never give up!